MW01380324

PLANTING SEADS

PLANTING SEADS

SOUTHEAST ASIAN ⬥ DIASPORA STORIES

CHANIDA PHAENGDARA POTTER
MK NGUYEN
NARATE KEYS
PHENG THAO

ISBN-13: 978-1-7327999-0-5

Library of Congress Catalog Number: 2018959726
Printed in the United States of America
First Printing: 2018
22   21   20   19   18   5   4   3   2   1

Book design by Christina Sayaovong Vang
christinavang.com

The SEAD Project
1007 West Broadway Avenue
Minneapolis, MN 55411

To order, visit **www.theseadproject.org.**

This book is made possible by the Minnesota Humanities Center through Minnesota Remembers Vietnam, an initiative led by Twin Cities PBS aimed at inspiring Minnesotans to remember, share stories, recognize bravery, express their reasons for dissent, and foster understanding around the lasting impact of war. TPT is partnering with the Minnesota Humanities Center to bring public conversations around these topics to communities across the state, thanks to support from the Arts and Cultural Heritage Fund that was created with a vote of the people of Minnesota on November 4, 2008.

To my parents Nouth and Phanh, my children Coraline Nakanya Dao
and Rohan Atith Issara, my husband Michael and my ancestors,
for their warmth and strength.
Chanida

To my grandmothers, Nguyễn Thi Kien and Nguyễn Thi Nghia, for
teaching me to be colorful but not flashy. To my beloved parents,
Nguyễn Thi Thanh and Nguyễn Minh Phan for being my first
teachers. To my sweethearts, Thaiphy and Stokely, for restructuring
my insides. To my siblings, Lam and Hoa for the profound and
often hilarious ways we translate our Việtness into English. To
my aunties, uncles and cousins, for teaching me to be like water
and showing the world that love and gratitude are quieter and far
stronger resources for resistance than anger. To the ancestors in our
lineage who labored to remove barriers and free space for future
generations to create new worlds.
mk

To my parents who survived the genocide and contribute their story
in this journey in recovery. To my son, Ethan Thoklasamon, my
daughter Braudara and my lifelong partner Eric Pick for your infinite
inspiration and support. Ar kun. To my sisters who love and support
my creative spirit. For my aunt Phalla Keo and my uncle Loeung Khi
who had contributed to my upbringing.
Narate

To the ancestors who taught us how to survive, be resilient and thrive
even when all we have left is just the will to live one more minute.
Pheng

TABLE OF CONTENTS

> "All wars are fought twice. The first time on the battlefield. The second time in memory."

Việt Thanh Nguyễn

Reclaimed images courtesy of Little Laos on the Prairie.

INTRODUCTION

There are more than 100,000 Hmong, Khmer, Lao and Việt diaspora who made Minnesota home since the resettlement period of 1975. For the Southeast Asian diaspora in Minnesota, our fragmented memories live in our minds and settle in our bodies like the wild grass on the midwest plains.

Southeast Asia has long been an object of colonial desire for its vast physical resources, from abundant lumber and vegetation to precious stones and fertile soil. It has attracted the French, Chinese, Dutch, Japanese, Russians and so many others over the centuries. But now we are turning the lens onto the most overlooked resource of Southeast Asia: her people. What are their inner dreams and stories? Why do they matter? The answers will be very personal to each reader but each story will leave you with a new understanding of our complex journeys.

We believe storytelling is necessary for us to start making sense of our being from the past, present and future. As part of the diaspora, our memories survived yet they're scattered definitions of who we are as a people, from a region known to the colonial imagination as Indochina, which has seen unimaginable devastation and is now adjusting to fast transformation of the socio-political forces that surrounds it. The stories in this book are a reflection of every aspect of our shared histories and who we are as a connected people that make up the complex Southeast Asian refugee diaspora in the United States.

There aren't many stories that center our people and the histories we hold that are about us, for us, by us. The Southeast Asian diaspora storytelling (SEADS) project wanted to change that by amplifying historically invisible Hmong, Khmer, Lao and Việt in Minnesota whose lives were impacted because of US military intervention. The project is a labor of love and challenges from a dedicated village of Southeast Asians who set out to reclaim and surface the less visible stories of our people. The driving forces of this project are led by Chanida Phaengdara Potter, mk nguyễn, Pheng Thao and Narate Keys; who hosted five community conversations with our respective communities across the Twin Cities. We created space for courageous and welcoming conversations about war, memory and what healing looks like for us.

This book is a culmination of year-long conversations and story collection from two generations of community members in their own words. Their stories contain sensitive, controversial, intimate and harrowing personal narratives, with interpretive poetry and art that represents us as the diaspora. These are 20 short stories from perspectives of veterans, scholars, activists, medics, mothers and young people who lived through French colonialism, the wars in Southeast Asia; also known to the American general public as the Vietnam War, to their resettlement beginnings on the Minnesota prairie.

The sweat, energy and careful attention put into this project and book; from the conversations to the book design to the storytellers; are all from our Southeast Asian communities. Our writers, translators and facilitators spent countless hours crafting and shaping these stories to honor the people who carry them. Through the process of collecting these stories; the prevalent themes of war, memory, history, family and healing emerged. As you page through this stunning book, understand the responsibility and power you hold with their truths and realities in the palms of your hands. There are more to these stories, but there is never enough room to fit them all nor do we claim its accuracy; just our communities speaking their truths and living their memories through today.

We are not historians or revisionists. We are young people rethinking what a just memory means for us in our path towards healing as a community with shared histories and journeys. Recovering memories requires us to sit and read the lived experiences of our people in these stories. We

(NY6-Feb. 15) FLOWERY WELCOME IN LAOS -- Vice President Hubert Humphrey receives a floral offering of welcome during his visit to Vientiane, capital of Laos, yesterday. On his 700-mile round trip to Laos, Humphrey inspected highway, dam and rural development projects. (AP Wirephoto by radio from Bangkok) (See AP Wire Story) (rh30730rca) 1966

believe there is beauty in our collective vulnerabilities and it's our hope that this book will spark and engage dialogue with those who continue to choose which narratives are dominant over our people's in mainstream pop culture.

While we wish we had the space in this book to include all of the wonderful intimate stories that were shared with us, know that this is only the first of many more to come. All stories will be honored online at www.theseadproject.org.

This book is intended to remind the world that we are more than our trauma, more than pain and more than our harm against each other as humans in the same struggle. We hope to lift understanding, reignite shared hope and inspire the next generation of Southeast Asians to not only remember what we have seen in our past, but to live in the present and to strive for a reimagined future together. This is just the beginning.

Women's
2017
Entered
High-School
2016-2017
·Declear as Theater
·Join AASA &
HNT

HMONG

"I am from Laos...So you are Lao?
No, I am Hmong.

I am from Thailand...So you are Thai?
No, I am Hmong.

My people are from China...So
Hmong people are actually Chinese?
No, we are Hmong."

Ze Thao

Hmong means "free"; a people who live freely based on their spiritual connection to land, air, water and all things in nature. A people who have often refused to be pushed to assimilate and acculturate wherever they have settled and been displaced. A people who have been resilient in their displacements and tribulations. A people who have been displaced for generations throughout much of their existence.

Hmong are indigenous people that have historically resided in various parts of China for over 5,000 years but because of forced assimilation some have been displaced to various parts of Southeast Asia. The group that settled in Laos experienced another onset of displacement when the Secret War broke out. The United States government recruited the Hmong to stop the Ho Chi Minh Trail that was running through Laos into Vietnam. The simultaneous Vietnam War dwarfed the war that was happening in Laos. Several hundreds, if not thousands of Hmong families had to flee Laos in fear of persecution for their participation with the United States. Many sought safety as refugees in Thailand by risking their lives crossing the Mekong River. From there their families were again separated to other parts of the world, many to the United States and eventually some to Minnesota. The first Hmong family arrived in Minnesota about 40 years ago. Since then many Hmong families arrived in Minnesota and migrated from other states to Minnesota because of family kinship.

Though the Hmong in Minnesota have been resilient in building a vastly diverse and progressive community many in the community still lack access to proper education, health care, food and meeting everyday basic needs. Poverty and low academic success are still very present in the community even though significant achievements have been made by a small subset of Hmong people. The Hmong in Minnesota have often been regarded by Hmong elsewhere in the country as leaders in building and shaping the Hmong community and identity here in the US.

The lack of progress is related to the trauma Hmong people have faced from generations of displacement, violence and wars that have been often left unaddressed. Much of this trauma remains invisible and hidden in the community and often manifests in the form of alcohol consumption; drug addictions; violence within the homes; depression; diabetes and other physical health problems; violence within the community and several more issues that weigh deeply on the lives of Hmong people living in Minnesota. The elders and those who were young enough to experience the war in Laos have often been silent in sharing their stories visibly. They are unsure of how to share the stories and revisit the memories of pain, horror, sorrow, hurt and lost loved ones. With these experiences left unaddressed, generations afterwards continue to be impacted by the traumas of war, violence

and pain of the community. Generational trauma is real and impacting generations of Hmong children and grandchildren. What happens when people are displaced and resettled in impoverished neighborhoods with little services and coping skills to help them manage their traumas; their main goal becomes survival.

In the five stories that are shared, each individual speaks of their experience related to war and trauma that they have experienced along with how they have come to be resilient not only for themselves but for their families and community. We share these stories not with the intent to re-traumatize people, but to share the strength of the community and lift up different narratives that have often been left out of the larger focus on the Vietnam War. These stories tell us that there were many things that happened during war. Military services members were not the only people directly impacted but an entire community was impacted and future generations were shaped by the aftermath of the war. We share these stories to honor our people and our ancestors who have taught us to survive and thrive. Our ancestors who have taught us what it means to be free. These stories teach us how Hmong is continually defined and re-defined.

Pheng Thao, Ze Thao and Bee Vang-Moua

KHMER

"To all the survivors out there, I want them to know that we are stronger and more resilient than we ever knew. We survived, that should be enough but it isn't. We must work hard to become whole again, to fill our soul with love and inspiration, to live the life that was intended for us before it was disrupted by war and horrors, and help rebuild a world that is better than the one we had just left."

Loung Ung

The Kingdom of Cambodia. Well known for its rich history and cultural traditions and the thousands of monuments and temples such as the iconic Angkor Wat and Bayon are what makes Cambodia truly one of the seven wonders of the world. The people of this great nation are called Khmer. Throughout Cambodia's history, the Khmer people have survived invasions from nearby countries and the French colonization during the late 1880's. In the middle of the 20th century, the rise of Communist groups were spreading over Southeast Asia and between 1969 and 1973, Cambodia was invaded by the United States and Vietnam due to the ongoing war, making more than 2 million Cambodians refugees. In 1975, the Khmer Rouge (Khmer Communist Party), led by Pol Pot, overthrew Cambodia to gain power and force Khmer people to be resettled to work in camps located in rural areas. During this time, approximately 1.7 million to 2.5 million Khmer people were executed, starved, and forced into labor which was more than one-fifth of the country population. Many Khmer refugees were able to escape to neighboring countries such as Thailand, but it wasn't until 1979 that the Khmer Rouge reign ended. According to the Minnesota Historical Society, in that year of 1979, there were approximately 150,000 refugees from Cambodia that immigrated to the United States. Today, Minnesota is the sixth largest Khmer population in the United States.

During the Khmer Rouge, all religious practices were banned. Today, about 95% of Khmer people are Buddhist. In the US, there are 275,000 people of Khmer heritage and in just Minnesota alone, there are over 10,000 people living in Minnesota. While that number may be small, we have one of the largest Cambodian Buddhist temples in North America called Watt Munisotram.

As we look towards the future, it's important that we share our own diaspora stories from our Khmer community. We are thankful and honored to have our Khmer community share their stories and support. The stories we collected come from many perspectives ranging from young adults to elders. These stories follow the lives of remarkable people and their own personal journey through the sacrifices and struggles of escaping persecution from Cambodia to living in Minnesota. Learning about what our families had to endure and how far our Khmer community has come to be where we are today has opened our eyes. Throughout this project, we all come from different parts of life, but the stories of our families are rooted in our hearts and minds forever.

Narate Keys and Sethey Ben

LAO

"A single seed can turn into a forest.
A single heart can transform a nation.
To be brave is jai ka.
To be generous is jai kwan."

Bryan Thao Worra

"To sleep is to not forget. Our dreams are left in the land we call home," said one Lao elder. It has often seemed like Laos never really lingered in the collective imagination of America until the debut of the recurring Lao character Kahn Souphanousinphone and his refugee family in the animated television series, *King of the Hill*. For Minnesotans, our history can be seen intertwining much earlier with the visit of Vice President Hubert H. Humphrey to Laos in February 1966. For most Lao, their journeys to the US began shortly after 1975, after the end of the Laotian Civil War, often referred to as "The Secret War" by historians; although it wasn't much of a secret to Congress or those in neighboring countries during the Vietnam War. By the end of 1975, along with our Viet and Khmer neighbors; almost 3,500 refugees from Laos were

approved by the U.S. Immigration and Naturalization Service to resettle in America, making us one of the largest migration of refugees to the States.

Despite over one hundred and sixty ethnicities identified in Laos, we've only just begun to hear from many, such as the Khmu, Tai Dam, Lue, and Iu Mien who were also refugees. The Lao Minnesotan community is considered the third largest population of Laotians in the US, after California and Texas. Some 492,000 of us in the US now trace our roots back to Laos, many from families allied with the US as part of a covert CIA army during the conflicts. Almost nine in ten of us lack college degrees, and many live below the Federal poverty line with untreated challenges of PTSD, depression, and other war traumas.

There are many stories we lose each year that could better inform our community of who we were, who we are, who we are becoming.

A recent PBS documentary series dedicated 18 episodes to the Vietnam War yet the Lao journey was all but completely excluded. Local communities emerged to create oral

histories of the war, however, many other stories of the Lao diaspora have not been heard, making the following stories we captured vital to the Lao Minnesotan history.

There are few who understand the journey of Lao veterans and their engagement with Minnesota veterans who were a part of the Southeast Asian conflicts.

As we look at the stories in this collection from the Lao community, we will see the perspectives of veterans, elders, teachers, artists, community organizers whose lives were shaped by being part of the diaspora. These truths that emerged were often those of perseverance and bravery as well as an indomitable human spirit determined to thrive. There are more stories to be told and shared, but these give us the courage to always remember first and to not retreat to invisibility and insignificance, but to seek each other and honor the people who carry these stories so that we can lay the foundations for the next generation of Lao dreamers.

Chanida Phaengdara Potter and Bryan Thao Worra

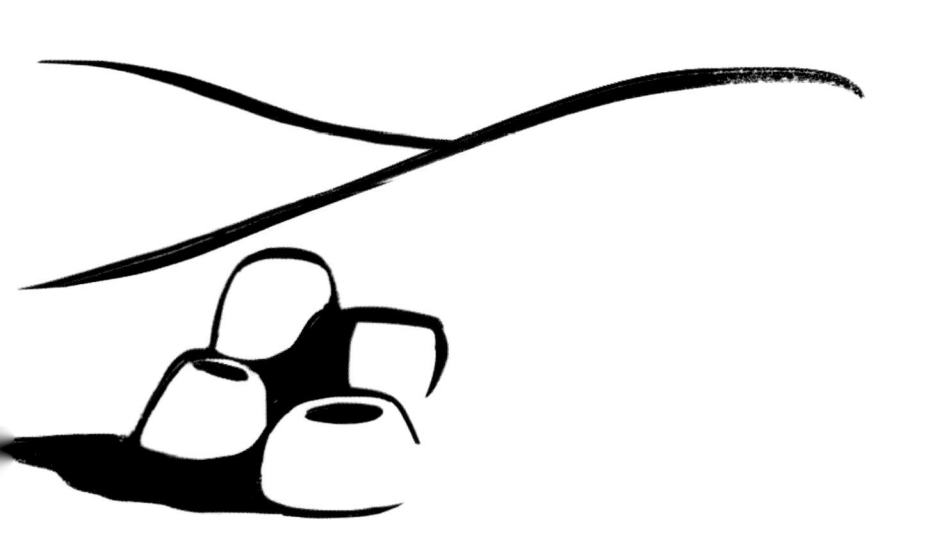

VIỆT

> "Vietnamese people have always been spoken word poets. How you say it is as important to the life of the word as the word itself."
>
> **Bao Phi**

This year cicadas rise above ground. They emerge from the mud in millions after 17 years of invisibility and silence. We can see their newly shed skin stuck on buildings. Day and night, we hear loud cicada sounds thickening the air, an unrelenting symphony reminding us that they are still here.

Việt people are still here and we want to welcome you into life with us. We are a small group of second generation Việts in Mni Sota who came together through the SEADS project. Together, we dare to step into emergence and create new pathways to name, ease, and shed the layers of pain and shame that constrict the ability of Việt people in Mni Sota to pay attention to and grow our instinctual practices towards wholeness and liberation. We know we are more than the stories that Hollywood and other people tell about us. We are ready to tell our own stories.

We start our journey with a small offering of five short stories from five remarkable first generation elders and peers who reflect on healing, memory recovery, and growing more spaces for Việt people in Mni Sota to cultivate hope, belonging, and the poetic vibrations of Việt love languages. The first generation shared their experience inside of war and their path towards healing from it. The more we talk

the more we sit with the multiplicity of truths inside of our complex story as diasporic Việts in Mni Sota.

The Việt body knows 1,110 years of Chinese and French colonization, Japanese occupation, and violent civil conflict. Việt earth was scorched by the United States. Fire zones, napalm, phosphorus, tear gas, and defoliants skinned flesh from her land and people. After the installment of new Socialist Republic of Việt Nam, a million South Việt Nam bodies were forced to live and work in reeducation camps and rural economic zones. The death toll inside the camp were estimated to be 165,000 people. Starting on April 30, 1975, two million Việts fled South Việt Nam. The body count of those who died during escape was over 500,000. Survivors scattered across five continents to grow life from past deaths. Now, over 1.5 million Việts are woven throughout small towns and major cities inside of the United States. Over 26,000 Việts now plant roots in Mni Sota soil.

The first generation spent 43 years seeding life in Mni Sota. We saw them create small community pockets, and patch resources together. They formed churches, temples, social organizations, and newspapers, and businesses to root

belonging across Việt people in Mni Sota. Inside our house, they taught children about Việt seeing, being and doing. As workers, we saw them labor arduously for others. As Việt Kieu, we saw them send money back home and manage family reunification processes.

As the second generation is now raising a third, we are ready to slow down, learn to listen, brave our truth, and deepen our connection with the first generation. Our hope from this small offering is to find the people who are looking for us. We hope this book reaches Việt people in Mni Sota who are interested in making new sounds, meanings, and pathways for Việts to to walk in right relationship with ourselves, others, and the planet. We know that our work together will create more breathing room for younger generations to shape and govern their lives free from colonial imagination.

mk nguyễn, Amanda Nguyễn and Lê Văn Tigana

OUR STORIES

Illustration by Leyen Trang

THE OLD MAN ON THE BRIDGE

Ông cụ trên cầu

*Sky Bui, 32
Saint Cloud

I come from Hue, one of the last ancient royal cities in Việt Nam. Growing up, I lived among fighters, sex workers, and gangsters. I remember being humiliated, bullied, hiding and being afraid of authority.

Before the war, I heard the stories of government officials knocking on people's doors, demanding confessions about their affiliations with the opposition. My grandparents' stories of war taught me that government officials were bad and could not be trusted. My own experiences fortified this lesson. I saw that people in government would say one thing and do another. So I began paying attention to what they did and not what they said.

When I was five years old, I asked my grandfather, "What if you weren't in Việt Nam?" Ever since, I have dreamt of other places. I pictured the United States (US) as a country of freedom, the land of dreams, and where everyone could live free from oppression. And when I was 12, that opportunity came. My aunt offered to sponsor my family's move to the US. Without hesitation, I took the opportunity immediately.

When I arrived in California, it was completely different from what I expected. I was lonely, betrayed by the false ideas of how great the US was. I remember my first few years in the US constantly hearing people saying, "Beggars will always be beggars." There was a time when my family brought me to a middle-school for enrollment, but I was rejected and told "to go back to your country." It had not been even a month in the US, and my relatives asked us to go home because they didn't want my family to become a burden to them.

So we were stuck with two choices: trying to survive in a place we did not feel welcomed or returning to a place I did not feel safe. So we moved. My family left California and moved to Minnesota, still holding strong to the conviction that one day I would prove them all wrong.

These were my first few years in the US. My family and I were on our own. As the older sister of four siblings, I promised to protect my family from anything or anyone who threatened to hold power over us. I watched my parents struggle to navigate the language barrier, so I studied hard to learn English, to stop the discrimination my family experienced on this new soil.

As a Buddhist, I believe in karma. We are all held accountable for the energy we put out in the world, at some point and in some form. I remember my grandparents telling stories to help me understand compassion, humility, and the moral lesson of helping people whenever I can.

As a child, I remember these stories guiding me to an old man on a bridge. This man was covered in lumps, and no one wanted to come near him. The man was sad, depressed, and suicidal. Remembering the lessons my family taught me, I decided to talk to this man. He was surprised that someone would be willing to talk to him. I kept speaking with him and over time, he was able to heal from his suffering. This memory made a strong impact on me, and it made me realize that I have the ability to help others heal.

As a survivor of verbal, physical, and mental abuse, and now a social worker, I help people pay attention to how pain affects our communities. I want us to see what abuse can look like and what effects it can have, especially to our children. Through this project, I have been working with elders and people in my generation to recover from the trauma they have faced.

Now, I am a mother. I reflect on the rich stories that my grandparents told me as a child. I am determined to teach my child the values that have been passed to me; that they can do what they set their mind to. They will learn that others will judge them and make them feel like they can't do what they want to do. I will tell my child about the resilience of our people, with a deep knowledge of wounds and sacrifice. They will learn that being young and Việt does not mean being inferior to anyone.

***Sky Bùi, 32
Saint Cloud**

Tôi đến từ Huế, thành phố cổ kính cuối cùng của triều đại phong kiến Việt Nam. Tôi lớn lên trong xóm nhỏ cùng những người lính, nạn mại dâm lẫn các thành phần phạm tội khác. Trong ký ức tuổi thơ của mình, tôi nhớ từng bị người khác sỉ nhục, ức hiếp, ẩn trốn, và sợ hãi nhà cầm quyền.

Trước chiến tranh, tôi nghe nhiều câu chuyện về các quan chức nhà nước gõ cửa nhà dân và yêu cầu người dân thú nhận liên quan với phe đối lập. Những câu chuyện từ ông ngoại về chiến tranh dạy cho tôi rằng quan chức nhà nước bất lương và không đáng tin cậy. Những trải nghiệm của bản thân càng cùng cố thêm niềm tin này. Tôi chú ý đến những gì họ làm, không phải những gì họ nói, và rút ra được kinh nghiệm rằng: quan chức nhà nước nói một đằng làm một nẻo.

Khi mới lên 5 tuổi, tôi hỏi ông ngoại "nếu ông ngoại không ở Việt Nam thì sẽ thế nào?" Từ đó, tôi thường mơ tưởng đến những vùng đất khác. Tôi hình dung Mỹ Quốc là đất nước của tự do, vùng đất của giấc mơ, và nơi mà tôi có thể sống tự do khỏi chế độ áp bức. Khi tôi lên 12 tuổi, cơ hội đến. Gia đình tôi được người dì ruột bảo lãnh sang Mỹ theo diện định cư. Tôi lập tức nắm lấy thời cơ không chút do dự.

Khi tôi đặt chân đến California, nó khác biệt với những gì mà tôi kỳ vọng. Tôi cảm thấy cô độc và bị phản bội bởi ý tưởng sai lầm về một Mỹ Quốc vĩ đại. Tôi nhớ lại khoảng thời gian đầu đến nước Mỹ đã nghe bạn bè của dì miệt thị: "ăn xin suốt đời chỉ là ăn xin". Khi gia đình làm hồ sơ đăng ký nhập học, tôi đã bị nhà trường từ chối và nói tôi hãy rời khỏi nước Mỹ và trở lại Việt Nam. Chưa đầy một tháng sau khi đến Mỹ, người thân bảo lãnh đề nghị gia đình tôi dọn ra vì không muốn gia đình tôi trở thành gánh nặng của họ.

Tôi cảm tưởng gia đình mình bị mắc kẹt giữa hai lựa chọn: sinh tồn tại nơi mà mình không được chào đón hoặc trở về nơi mà mình không có cảm giác an toàn. Gia đình tôi rời California và dọn đến Minnesota cùng hoài bão và niềm tin rằng một ngày nào đó tôi sẽ chứng minh với những kẻ hoài nghi là họ đã sai.

"Chẳng có ai đến giúp chúng ta cả!". Những năm đầu trên đất Mỹ, gia đình tôi đơn độc. Tôi có 4 anh chị em, là chị của 2 đứa em gái, tôi phải bảo vệ em mình trước tất cả những kẻ nào muốn ức hiếp chúng. Chứng kiến cảnh ba mẹ mình gặp nhiều trắc trở vì không biết tiếng, tôi quyết tâm phải học tiếng Anh thật giỏi và chăm chỉ để giúp gia đình ngừng bị kỳ thị và trụ vững tại đất Mỹ.

Là một Phật tử, tôi tin vào Nhân-Quả. Tại một thời điểm nào đó và dưới một dạng nào đó, tất cả chúng ta sẽ chịu trách nhiệm với những gì chúng ta làm. Nhớ lại những câu chuyện được nghe kể từ ông bà ngoại giúp tôi hiểu hơn về lòng trắc ẩn, sự sỉ nhục, và hình thành bản năng giúp đỡ người khác bất cứ khi nào có thể.

Tôi quay trở lại hồi ức tuổi thơ của mình về một ông lão bên chiếc cầu. Ông lão mà chẳng có ai muốn đến gần chỉ vì lưng gù của ông. Ông lão buồn, trầm cảm, và muốn quyên sinh. Nhớ đến những bài học nhân văn từ gia đình mình, tôi quyết định đến trò chuyện cùng ông. Ông lão kinh ngạc khi thấy rằng có ai đó sẵn lòng đến với ông. Tôi tiếp tục đến những ngày sau đó nữa và nhận ra rằng ông lão dường như với bớt nhiều khổ đau. Điều này đã tác động mạnh đến tôi, giúp tôi nhận ra rằng tôi có khả năng giúp người khác chữa lành vết thương trong lòng họ.

Từ kinh nghiệm bị ngược đãi của chính mình và nay đã trở thành một nhân viên chăm sóc sức khỏe tinh thần, tôi giúp người Việt nhận ra tầm ảnh hưởng của sức lan toả nỗi đau qua nhiều thế hệ trong khắp cộng đồng người Việt. Tôi muốn cộng đồng người Việt hiểu rõ hơn về hành vi ngược đãi đặc biệt đối với trẻ em. Qua chương trình này, tôi đang làm việc với thế hệ lớn tuổi cũng như với thế hệ trẻ để cùng nhau khôi phục, nuôi nấng nhân cách của nòi giống Việt.

Giờ đây tôi đã là mẹ. Tôi soi chiếu những câu chuyện mà ông bà đã kể với mình khi còn thơ bé trên cuộc đời của chính mình. Tôi quyết tâm dạy dỗ con mình rằng: "Con có thể hoàn thành bất cứ điều gì nếu con đặt tâm trí vào, và đừng để tác động bởi những phán xét của người khác mà không đạt được ước mơ của mình. Con đến từ giòng giống Việt, tổ tiên con là những người có khả năng hồi phục từ bất cứ vết thương nào. Con sẽ hãnh diện vì tuổi trẻ và nòi giống Việt của mình không thua kém bất cứ ai." Tôi muốn giáo dục chúng có một ý thức sâu sắc về sự tổn thương và lòng hy sinh.

Name and identifiers have been changed under storyteller's request.

i was born

THE LAO PROFESSOR

ສາດສະດາຈານຄົນລາວ

Banlang Phoummasouvanh, 72
Eagan

Banlang was born in the northern town of Sam Neua, Laos and grew up in Phon Hong, Vientiane province. She is a retired educator, with more than 30 years of teaching ESL and Social Studies to English language learners in the Minneapolis Public School District.

Images courtesy of Banlang Phoummasouvanh

I was born at the end of the French Union and grew up with a father who was a political figure and eventually became the governor of Phon Hong District in Vientiane Province. Lao people had two sides. One side wanted the French to no longer oppress our people. One side wanted the French to stay because they had livelihoods and would feel lost without them there. The locals would only teach Lao language, classics and culture but topics such as sciences, philosophy and social studies were all taught by the French. After the collapse of colonialism, the French military left and only a handful of diplomats and educators stayed behind to help us transition at the university. After '75, the schools wanted to erase French presence in the curriculum. But they couldn't keep up with it. So then we learned Russian, Chinese and Việt Namese. Any country that came to influence Laos, we'd learn how to speak their language.

My father moved to many different corners of Laos to work. I studied literature at Université de Bordeaux in France for nine years and then studied at Southern Illinois University in '72 where I got my teaching license. I taught at Dong Dok University until the end of the war. That's when they started taking my colleagues one by one to the labor camps, to teach our people the new communist ways. The university faculty were slowly being convinced that the communist ideology was the only path towards liberation and that the monarchy had to end its rule. Some would regret it. While some say it's what's needed in Laos.

They said Americans brainwashed us as educators who studied abroad. My family was worried that my academic days in America would be a threat against my safety in Laos, so they encouraged me to leave the country. I had to leave everything behind. Even my children were separated from me. All I had on was my sarong and a handful of cash. I didn't want to seem suspicious to the military, so I pretended I was a poor farm girl seeking food along the Mekong but I took a boat to Nong Khai, Thailand with my youngest daughter and waited for my brother to bring my oldest daughter. I prayed and prayed that we'd be reunited. Buddha answered and we found each other at a secret spot in Nong Khai. My decision to leave Laos broke my heart. Many of my family members were already being rounded up and taken to the labor camps and I was warned I would be next. I told myself I didn't do anything wrong. loved my country, so why would they do this to me? I had to think about the well-being of my two daughters first.

We settled in the midwest. I was a seamstress in Sioux City, Iowa in my first few years. After moving to Minneapolis, I did social work at a city clinic, helping interpret for Lao clients who couldn't work and sought therapy for their PTSD and depression. As I learned about the struggling lives that poor Lao people had to adjust to in Minneapolis, I couldn't help but cry in front of the psychiatrist to help my people.

ບັນລັງ ພິມມະສຸວັນ, ອາຍຸ 72 ປີ
Eagan

ບັນລັງ ກຳເນີດທີ່ທາງພາກເໜືອຂອງເມືອງຊຳເໜືອ, ສປປ ລາວ, ແລະ ເຕີບໃຫຍ່ຢູ່ ເມືອງໂພນໂຮງ, ແຂວງວຽງຈັນ. ປະຈຸບັນ ບັນລັງ ເປັນພະນັກງານບຳນານ ເຊິ່ງມີປະສົບການດ້ານການສຶກສາ, ທ່ວງກວ່າ 30 ປີ ໃນການສອນການກະກຽມພາສາອັງກິດ (English Second Language) ແລະ ສັ່ງຄົມສາດ ໃຫ້ແກ່ນັກຮຽນທີ່ກຳລັງກຽມພາສາອັງກິດ ຢູ່ເມືອງມິນິເອັນໂປລິສ.

ຂ້າພະເຈົ້າກຳເນີດໃນຄຸວງຕອນທ້າຍຂອງ ສະທະພາບຝຣັ່ງເສດ ແລະ ພໍ່ຂອງຂ້າພະເຈົ້າເອງກໍເປັນນັກກາບານ ເມືອງ ແລະ ໄດ້ຮັບໜ້າທີ່ເປັນເຈົ້າເມືອງ, ເມືອງໂພນໂຮງ, ແຂວງວຽງຈັນ. ຄົນລາວນັ້ນສະໄໝນັ້ນມີ ຄວາມຄິດສອງແບບ ຫຼື ສອງຈິດໃຈ: ໃຈຜີ່ງຢາກໃຫ້ ສະທະພາບຝຣັ່ງເສດ ອອກໄປຈາກປະເທດລາວເພາະ ບໍ່ຢາກຖຶກກົດຂີ່ອີກຕໍ່ໄປ ແລະ ອີກໃຈຜີ່ງ ຢາກໃຫ້ຢູ່ເພາະເຂົາເຈົ້າບໍ່ຮູ້ຈະເຮັດແບບໃດຕໍ່ໄປກັບຊິວິດ ການເປັນຢູ່ ຖ້າພວກເຂົາຢູ່ແລ້ວ. ການສອບຫັ້ງສິ ຫຼື ວິຊາຕ່າງໆໃຫ້ປະຊາຊົນ ໃນຍຸກສະໄໝນັ້ນ ກໍລ້ວນແຕ່ສອບ ພາສາລາວ, ປະຫວັດສາດ ແລະ ອັດທະບະທຳ; ສ່ວນວິຊາອື່ນໆກໍມີ: ຊີວະສາດ, ປັດຊະຍາ, ສັ່ງຄົມສາດ ແມ່ນຈະສອບໂດຍຄົນຝຣັ່ງ. ພາຍຫຼັງການລົບລ້າງໄລເຫີ່ລ່າເມືອງຂຶ້ນ, ທະຫານຝຣັ່ງໄດ້ກັບ ຄືນປະເທດ ແລະ ເຫຼືອແຕ່ນັກການທູດ ແລະ ຄູອາຈານ ທີ່ຍັງຢູ່ໃຫ້ການຊ່ວຍເຫຼືອພວກເຮົາ ໃນການເຂົ້າບັນຈຸໃນມະຫາວິທະຍາໄລ. ຫຼັງຈາກປີ 1975, ໂຮງຮຽນທັງຫຼາຍພະຍາຍາມລົບລ້າງພາສາ ຝຣັ່ງອອກຈາກລະບົບການສຶກສາ ແຕ່ກັບເອົາພາສາອື່ນໆຂຶ້ນ: ພາສາລັດເຊຍ, ພາສາຈີນ ແລະ ພາສາຫວຽດນາມ ມາສິດສອບ ຫຼື ເຂົ້າໃນລະບົບການສຶກສາ ແທນຍ້ອນປະເທດຄັ່ງກ່າວມີອິດທິພົນທີ່ພຶບທຍາຍ ໃນສະໄໝນັ້ນ ແລະ ມີຄວາມຈຳເປັນ ບໍ່ຕ້ອງໄດ້ຮຽນເອົາພາສາເພີ່ມ.

ໄລຍະຕໍ່ມາພໍ່ຂອງຂ້າພະເຈົ້າເອງກໍໄດ້ຍ້າຍໄປຫຼາຍບ່ອນເພື່ອຊອກວຽກ ເຮັດງານທຳ. ຂ້າພະເຈົ້າເອງໄດ້ ເຂົ້າຮຽນຢູ່ເມືອງບໍຣໍໂດ, ປະເທດຝຣັ່ງເສດ ເພື່ອສຶກສາກ່ຽວກັບອັນມະຕະຄືເປັນເວລາ 9 ປີ ແລະ ສຶກ ສາຕໍ່ເພື່ອຍາດ ແຍ່ງເອົາໃນອະນຸຍາດການການສອບ ຢູ່ມະຫາວິທະຍາໄລ ເຂົ້າເຕີມ ອິລິນອຍ ໃນປີ 1972. ຂ້າພະເຈົ້າໄດ້ສອບຫັ້ງສິຢູ່ ມະຫາວິທະຍາໄລດັ່ງໂດຍ ຈົບຖອດເວລາສິ້ນສຸດສິ່ງຄາມ. ໃນຄຸວງເວລານັ້ນ, ເພື່ອນຮ່ວມງານຂອງຂ້າພະເຈົ້າກໍໄດ້ຖຶກກັກໂຕໄປຄ້າຍແຮງງານເທື່ອລະຄົນ, ເພື່ອຝຶກສອບພວກເຮົາກ່ຽວກັບລະບອບຄອມມູນິດ. ພ້ອມໝູ່ກັນ, ມະຫາວິທະຍາໄລຕ່າງໆກໍຖຶກຊັກຈູງ ແລະ ປ່ຽນລັດທິມາ ເປັນຄອມມູນິດເຊັ່ນໆຍວງກັນ, ຍ້ອນເຫດຜົນທີ່ວ່າ ຖ້າຍ

ໆກບິດປ່ອຍທິດສະລະພາບແມ່ນຕ້ອງໄດ້ປະຕິກ໌ມ ລະບອບລາວຊາທິປະໄຕ. ບາງຈຳນອນເທິ່ນຕິ ແລະ ຄິດວ່າເປັນທາງອອກທີ່ດີຕໍ່ປະເທດລາວ ແລະ ຄົນພັດບໍ່ ເທິ່ນຕິ ແລະ ຄິດກັບແຫຼງໆກັບການກະທຳດັ່ງກ່າວ.

ທຼາຍໆຄົນກໍກ່າວໃຈໂຈມຕິວ່າພວກເຮົາຜູ້ທີ່ໄດ້ໄປສຶກສາຢູ່ຕ່າງປະເທດນັ້ນແມ່ນ ບໍຕຶກອາເມລິກາລ້າງສະໝອງ ແລ້ວ, ເຊິ່ງນັ້ນ ເຮັດໃຫ້ຄອບຄົວຂອງຂ້າພະ ເຈົ້າກັງວົນ ແລະ ເປັນທ່ວງທຼາຍຕໍ່ກັບຄວາມປອດໄພຂອງ ຂ້າພະເຈົ້າທຼາຍ ຍ້ອນແບບນັ້ນ, ເຂົາເຈົ້າຈຶ່ງໄດ້ສະໜັບສະໜຸນຂ້າພະເຈົ້າໃຫ້ອອກຈາກປະເ ທດໃນເວລາ ນັ້ນເພື່ອຄວາມປອດໄພ. ຂ້າພະເຈົ້າໄດ້ຖິ້ມທຸກຢ່າງທີ່ມີ, ລູກໆ ແລະ ຂ້າພະເຈົ້າເອງກໍຕ້ອງໄດ້ແຍກກັນຢູ່. ຂ້າພະເຈົ້າບໍ່ມີທຍບຕິດຕົວເລີຍ, ມີພຽງຜ້າສີ້ນ ແລະ ເຖິງຈຳນອບພຶ່ງ, ແລະ ເພື່ອໃຫ້ເປັນການສົ່ງໃສ, ຂ້າພະເຈົ້າຈຶ່ງຕ້ອງໄດ້ປອມໂຕເປັນແມ່ຍິງ ພ້ອມລູກນ້ອຍຕິດມານຳ ພອມກຳລັງອອກຊອກທາ່ອາຫາບຕາມ ແຖມແມ່ບ້ານຂອງ ໃນເວລາໄດ້ໂອ ກາດເພາະກໍເລີຍລັກຂີ່ເຮືອຂ້າມໄປ ເມືອງພະວຄງກາຍ, ປະເທດໄທ. ເມື່ອ ໄປຮອດທາງພຸ້ນ ຂ້າພະເຈົ້າກໍໄດ້ແຕ່ຫຼ້າມື້ທີ່ຄອບຄົວຈະໄດ້ກັບໜ້າ, ແລະ ຖ້າໃຫ້ອ້າຍຂອງຂ້າພະເຈົ້າ ເອົາລູກສາວກໍພາຂ້າພະເຈົ້າຂ້າມມາ ແລະ ໃນທີ່ສຸດພະພຸດທະເຈົ້າກໍເທິ່ນໃຈ ແລະ ໃຫ້ພວກຂ້າພະເຈົ້າ ເຈິກັບອິກຄັ້ງທີ່ ພະວຄງກາຍ. ການຕັດສິນໃຈໜີອອກຈາກປະເທດລາວ ເປັນການຕັດສິນໃຈທີ່ຍາກທີ່ສຸດ, ແຕ່ຂ້າພະເຈົ້າມີຄວາມຈຳເປັນຕ້ອງຮັບຍ້ອນສ ະຖານະການເກີນບັງຄັບ ແລະ ຄົນໃນຄອບຄົວຂ້າພະເຈົ້າ ບາງຄົນກໍຖຶກຄຸກກັກໂຕ ປໍຄ້າຍແຮງງານທີ່ແລ້ວ. ຂ້າພະເຈົ້າອກໂຕເອງຕະທຼອດເວລາວ່າ ຂ້າພະເຈົ້າບໍ່ໄດ້ ເຮັດທຍັງຜິດ; ຂ້າພະເຈົ້າຮັກປະເທດຊາດ, ເປັນທຍັງເຂົາເຈົ້າຈຶ່ງຕ້ອງເຮັດແບບ ນັ້ນນຳພວກຂ້າພະເຈົ້າດ້ວຍ ແຕ່ເພື່ອຄວາມປອດໄພ ແລະ ປົກປ້ອງຊິວິດການເປັ ນຢູ່ຂອງລູກສາວຂອງຄົນ ຂ້າພະເຈົ້າຈຶ່ງໄດ້ໜີອອກມາ ໃຫ້ພັ້ນຈາກສິ່ງອັນຕະລ າຍເທື່ອນັ້ນ.

ໃນຊ່ວງສາມປີທຳທິດ, ພວກເຮົາໄດ້ລົງຫຼັກປັກຖານຢູ່ພາກເໜືອ, ແລະ ຂ້າພະເຈົ້າໄດ້ປະກອບອາຊິບເປັນ ຊ່າງຫຍິບເຄື່ອງຢູ່ ເມືອງ ຊູ, ລັດໄອໂອວາ. ພາຍຫຼັງທີ່ໄດ້ຍ້າຍໄປຢູ່ ເມືອງມິນິເອັນໂປລິຄ, ຂ້າພະເຈົ້າໄດ້ ບັນຈຸເຮັດວຽກກ່ຽວກັບວຽກສັ່ງຄົມສົງເຄາະ ຢູ່ ຄລິນິກໃນຕົວເມືອງ, ຊ່ວຍແປພາສາ ແລະ ອຳນວຍຄວາມ ສະດວກຕ່າງໆໃຫ້ກັບຄົນລາວທີ່ບໍ່ສາມາດເຮັດວຽກ ແລະ ຕ້ອງການການຊ່ວຍເຫຼືອທາງດ້ານການ ບຳບັດໂລກຄວາມຍຸດທັ້ງ ໆຈາກມົລະສຸມຊິວິດ ແລະ ຄວາມເສົ້າສະທຶດຕ່າງໆ. ເວລາທີ່ຂ້າພະເຈົ້າ ເທິບຄົນລາວຕິດທຸກໄດ້ຍາກ ແລະ ພະຍາຍາມປັບຕິວໃຫ້ເຂົ້າກັບຊິວິດໃໝ່ຢູ່ ເມືອງມິນິເອັນໂປລິຄ, ຂ້າພະເຈົ້າເອງກໍຄິດບໍ່ອິດຄົບ ແລະ ສິ່ງສາບ ບໍ່ໄດ້ ບາງຄັ້ງກໍ ນ້ຳຕາຕິກຕໍ່ໜ້ານັກຈິດຕະແພດທີ່ກຳລັງຊ່ວຍ ເຫຼືອເຂົາເຈົ້າຢູ່.

The Fall of Saigon/Liberation
Ngày Giải phóng miền Nar

1975

Past-197

CHAO FA HMONG RESISTANCE

Caub Fab:
Hmoob Kev Tawm Tsam

Neng Shao Yang, 60
Saint Paul

Image courtesy of Neng Shao Yang

My home village is Long Moune in the province of Xieng Khouang, Laos. My ancestors had lived there for at least 200 years. I was born in 1958 into a large family. My father had two wives. My step mother had 6 girls, no sons, and my mom had 7 boys, no girls. My parents passed away when I was only two years old so I don't have any memory of them or remember how they looked. Before they passed we were a wealthy family, but as orphans, we were poor. In 1962, my three older brothers joined General Vang Pao's CIA guerilla force for food and shelter. In 1965, I began year one of Lao school and stayed all the way up to year six.

I remember having to memorize French phrases on the chalkboard: le maison, en enfant. In 1970, my brother got married, so for one year I enlisted in Vang Pao's troops and became his replacement when I was only 12 years old. Because I was young I wasn't allowed to do much. I filled water, handled food, and cleaned up after the soldiers. In 1971, I went back to school in Vientiane. I almost finished my diploma, but in May 1975 it felt like the world changed and turned upside down. There was no hope. I had to return to my village to meet up with my family. It took a car ride and then a whole day's walk before reaching hope.

Do you know about Chao Fa? It means Hmong resistance, but the communist deemed us jungle rebels.

Hmong are not jungle people. We have always been highlanders, but we became a target. At night we heard the village dogs bark at the communists. They captured people in the dark and in the morning we discovered their lifeless bodies at the farms. They called us losers of the war to justify what they did to us. We didn't have a choice but to run into the jungles. We, Chao Fa, emerged as a means for survival. We needed to escape from nyab la, communists. We referred to all communists as nyab la, Việt, but they weren't all Việt. At the time, anyone who was communist was called nyab la (there were Hmong communists too) - we didn't have another word for them in our language.

In our hearts we didn't want to be Chao Fa but staying in the village was hopeless. In the jungles we had to Lai Thai, vigilantly protect ourselves. We came together to po pua, share secret intel and help each other sneak out of the jungle to Thailand. Whenever we could, we quickly dug up yams to eat. We saw dead Hmong people alongside the path to get to the rendezvous point. They died from injuries and starvation. My brother, Txos, stepped on a landmine and we knew he wouldn't be able to keep up. We covered him with a blanket and left him with a gun then continued onward to the Mekong. We crossed the Mekong by 1980 with 50 people. Almost everything was thrown away to lighten our cargo. I was wearing a pair of loose shorts and nothing else. Once we crossed, we waited until word was sent to our relatives and they brought us clothes and shoes.

From 1981 - 1988 I worked with World Vision as a camp medic and supervisor. I ordered IVs, checked people's vitals, and was in charge of food inventory and distribution. In 1994, my family and I came to the United States. By 1997 I obtained my GED and went on to college to become an EMT/paramedic. I graduated and became one of the first Hmong paramedics in the Twin Cities. However, I'm a small person, and working as an EMT was difficult. Eventually, I stopped working as an EMT and became an entrepreneur. I owned and operated a liquor store in Plymouth until I sold it in 2007. Now, I run a senior adult day care center in Minneapolis.

—

Neej Som Yaj, 60
Saint Paul

Kuv lub zej lub zog hu ua Long Moune nyob rau xeev Xieng Khouang, Nplog teb. Kuv pog koob yawg koob twb nyob ntawv tau ob puas xyoo dhau los lawm. Kuv yug rau xyoo 1958, rau ib tse neeg coob heev. Kuv txiv muaj ob tug poj niam. Kuv niam yau muaj rau tus ntxhais, tiam sis tsis muaj tub. Kuv niam, uas yog niam loj, muaj peb xya leej tub, tiam sis ho tsis muaj ib tug ntxhais li. Kuv niam thiab kuv txiv nkawv tau tag sim neej thaum kuv nyuam qhuav muaj ob xyoos xwb. Vim li ntawv, kuv yeej tsis nco thiab cim tsis tau tlas nkawv zoo li cas. Ua ntej nkawv xiam, peb kuj yog ib tse neeg uas muaj nyiaj nplua nuj thiab, tiam sis thaum peb los ua ntsuag peb cia li txom nyem lawm. Nyob rau xyoo 1962, kuv peb tug tij laug hlob tau mus ua tub nrog rau Nai Phoo Vaj Pov thiab CIA (Central Intelligence Agency) pab Special Guerrila Unit (SGU), kom peb thiaj tau zaub mov thiab lub chaw nyob. Tom qab ntawv rau xyoo 1965, kuv tau mus kawm ntawv xyoo ib rau ib lub tsev kawm ntawv Nplog. Kuv tau kawm ntawv tau rau xyoo ntxiv.

Kuv tseem nco tau hais tias peb tau raug cim cov lus Fabkis nyob rau daim kab das: le maison, en enfant. Nyob rau xyoo 1970, kuv ib tug tij laug tau yuav poj niam. Kuv, uas muaj 12 xyoos xwb, thiaj li tau mus hloov nws, mus ua Nai Phoo Vaj Pov ib tug tub rog tau ib lub xyoos nkaus. Vim kuv tseem yau heev, lawv kuj tsis pub kuv ua dab tsi ntau. Kuv tsuas ce dej, saib thiab ua zaub ua mov, thiab tu tej chaw uas cov tub rog tsis nyob lawm. Nyob rau xyoo 1971, kuv tau rov qab mus kawm ntawv ntxiv rau hauv lub nroog Vientiane. Kuv twb kawm yuav tiav kuv daim Diploma, tiam sis thaum lub 5 hlis ntuj, xyoo 1975 ntawv, zoo li lub ntiaj teb tau tig, hloov rov qab rov quav lawm. Kuv yeej tsis muaj kev cia siab li lawm. Kuv yuav tsum tau rov qab mus rau kuv lub zos mus cuag kuv tsev neeg xwb xwb. Kuv tau caij tsheb ces mam li taug ib hnub ke, kuv mam li mus txog kuv txoj kev cia siab.

Koj puas paub txog Caub Fab? Ntawm peb Hmoob, Caub Fab yog peb cov Hmoob uas nyob hav zoov, tiv thaiv lub teb lub chaw thiab tawm tsam cov Communist. Tiam sis ntawm cov Communist, peb ces tsuas yog lawv tus yeeb ncuab nyob nkaum rau hav zoov hav tsuag xwb.

Peb Hmoob yeej ib txwm tsis yog neeg nyob rau hav zoov hav tsuag. Ib txwm peb yeej nyob toj roob hauv pes, tiam sis luag tau tsom peb tua. Thaum tsaus ntuj, peb tau hnov aub nthe cov Communists. Lawv tau tuaj tsom ntes, khi tib neeg coj mus lawm. Tos tag kis lub hnub tawm xwb, mus saib tom teb ces mam li pom cov neeg ntawv lub cev tuag pov ua lwj ua liam. Cov Communists tau hais tias lawv tau ua li ntawv vim peb yog cov swb tsov nrog lawm. Tsis muaj hau kev lawm, peb thiaj li yuav tsum tau mus khiav nkaum rau hauv hav zoov hav tsuag. Peb txoj kev ua Caub Fab tau tshwm sim los ntawm peb khiav txoj kev tuag. Peb yuav tsum tau khiav kom dim cov Nyab Laj, losis Communists. Tus twg uas yog Communists ces peb yeej muab hu ua Nyab Laj, tiam sis Communists tsis yog nyab laj nkaus nkaus xwb. Kuj muaj Hmoob uas yog Communists thiab. Rau peb lawv kuj yog Nyab Laj thiab, vim peb Hmoob tsis muaj lus los tis rau lawv lawm.

Nyob hauv peb lub siab peb yeej tsis xav ua Caub Fab, tiam sis vim nyob hauv zos los tsis muaj kev cia siab li lawm. Hauv hav zoov hav tsuag, peb yuav tsum tau los sis siv dag zog thiab tawm tswv yim los tiv thaiv peb tus kheej. Peb tau los ua ke los sis los tawm thiab qhia tswv yim kom peb dim hauv hav zoov hav tsuag hla mus rau sab Thaib. Yog thaum twg peb muaj sib hawm ces peb khawb qos los noj. Thaum peb taug kev mus rau qhov chaw sib ntsib, peb tau pom Hmoob tau tuag rau tej ntug kev. Tej tug ces tuag vim kev raug mob. Hos tej tug ces tau tuag vim txoj kev yoo tshaib yoo nqhis. Kuv tus tij laug Txos tau los tsuj raug ib lub mem. Thaum nws tsuj raug tag ces peb yeej paub lawm tias nws yuav mus tsis taus nrog peb lawm. Peb thiaj li tau muab ib daim pam los npog nws thiab ib rab phom rau nws xwb ces peb mus lawm. Peb rau siab ntso mus kom txog tus dej Nab Khoom. Peb 50 leej kuj los hla dhau tus dej Nab Khoom rau xyoo 1980. Peb cov nra ces raug tso pov tseg tag nyob rau sab Nplog vim nkoj thauj tsis taus. Kuv ces twb tsis muaj dab tsi hnav li, tsuas yog hnav ib lub ris luv lawm xwb. Peb tau los tos kom neeg xa xov mus rau peb cov kwv tij Hmoob uas twb los tim Thaib teb ua ntej lawm. Peb cov kwv tij Hmoob mam li nqa me ris me tsho tuaj rau peb hnav.

Nyob rau xyoo 1981 txog xyoo 1988, kuv tau ua hauj lwm nrog World Vision. Kuv tau los yog ib tug kws muab tshuaj thiab tus saib xyuas peb lub Yeej Thoj Nam Tawg Rog. Kuv yog tus los yuav cov IV (Intravenous), kuv tau kuaj tib neeg tej hlab ntsha seb puas xim yeem, thiab kuv kuj tau los tuav peb lub Yeej Thoj Nam tej zaub mov thiab kev faib zaub mov rau sawv daws. Nyob rau xyoo 1994, kuv tsev neeg peb tau tuaj rau lub teb chaws Meskas. Kuv kawm tiav kuv daim GED (General Educational Development) rau xyoo 1997, ces kuv tau mus kawm ntxiv nrau tsev kawm ntawv qib siab, mus ua ib tug EMT/paramedic. Tom qab kuv kawm tiav, kuv tau los yog thawj thawj tus Hmoob uas yog paramedic nyob rau lub Nroog Ntxaib no. Tiam sis vim kuv yog ib tug neeg me, kuv txoj hauj lwm paramedic tau nyuab zog rau kuv lawm. Tsis ntev xwb, kuv kuj tau tso kuv txoj hauj lwm tseg es los ua ib tug tub ua lag ua luam lawm. Kuv tau kav ib lub khw muag dej caw nyob rau Plymouth txog ntua thaum kuv muab muag rau xyoo 2007. Tam sim no, kuv tuav ib lub tsev kaj siab rau neeg laus nyob rau Minneapolis.

"If leaves don't shed, the forest can't feel the light."

Hmong Proverb

LOSS IN CAMBODIA

ការឈឺចាប់ និងការវេទនា នៅកម្ពុជា

Lar Mundstock, 75
Saint Paul

Image courtesy of Lar Mundstock

My name is Lar. I was a high school professor in Cambodia in the mid-sixties a survivor of the mass genocide of Pol Pot's radical communist regime from 1975 to 1979, where one-third of the population died from execution, slave labor, famine, and diseases. I was one of the few survivors of Easterners (Bophea) sent to be executed in the Northern region (Pursat Province) in October 1978.

I faced the failure of an escape attempt in June 1979, when the Thai government forced the refugees to return to Cambodia through Chain Dangrek. I had to walk across minefields without food and water amongst thousands of desperate and disappointed refugees. Many of them died.

I experienced the deepest sorrow and suffering for the loss of my country and loved ones. I cried desperately from the great fear and pain I felt inside and hoped for some sign of help. Any tiny mental, spiritual or material support was worth millions of dollars. I prayed to every god, to every spirit to help me escape the horrors that haunted me.

I arrived in the United States in September 1980, in Eugene, Oregon and then moved to Minnesota in December 1980. I earned my Bachelors of Arts from the Metropolitan State University in Minnesota in 1991. I became very instrumental in representing my fellow Cambodian women and appeared as a community leader and was actively involved in several Cambodian non-profit organizations.

I became a co-founder of the Cambodian Students of Minnesota and a founder of Association of Minnesota (UCAM). I served as an executive director since November 1990, when my predecessor, Meng Kruy Ung had to resign due to illness and passed away a year later.

One of his poems "Left Mothers Behind to Guard the City" inspired me and I committed myself to become a role model to my country, my people; in order to strive to become the good children of Cambodia to respond to every mother's plea for my nation.

———

ឡា មុនសុក, 75
Saint Paul

ខ្ញុំឈ្មោះឡា។ ខ្ញុំគឺជាអតីតគ្រូបង្រៀនសាលាមធ្យមសិក្សានៅកម្ពុជា ក្នុងពាក់កណ្ដាលនៃឆ្នាំហុកសិប ជាអ្នកនៅរស់ពីការប្រល័យពូជសាសន៍ នៃរបបកុម្មុយនិស្សរបស់ប៉ុល ពត ចាប់តាំងពីឆ្នាំ 1975 ដល់ 1979 ដែលប្រជាជនមួយភាគបី បានស្លាប់ដោយសារការប្រហារជីវិត ទាសករពលកម្ម ការអត់បាយ និងជំងឺនានា។ ខ្ញុំជាមនុស្សម្នាក់ ក្នុងចំណោមនៃអ្នកនៅរស់ នៅភាគខាងកើត (ឬពាំ) ដែលគេបានបញ្ជូន ទៅឲ្យប្រហារជីវិត នៅភូមិភាគខាងជើង (ខែត្រពាំងតិសាត់) ក្នុងខែតុលា 1978។

ខ្ញុំបានប្រឈមមុខនូវបរាជ័យនៃការរៀបសង្សា ដែលបានប៉ុនប៉ងធ្វើក្នុងខែមិថុនា 1979 នៅពេលដែលរដ្ឋាភិបាលថៃ បានបង្ខំជនរៀបសង្សា ឲ្យវិលត្រឡប់ទៅកម្ពុជាវិញ តាមរយៈជួរភ្នំដងរែក។ ខ្ញុំត្រូវដើរឆ្លងកាត់ចំការមីន ដោយគ្មានស្បៀងអាហារ និងទឹកជឹក ក្នុងបណ្ដាជនរៀបសង្សារាប់ពាន់នាក់ ដែលស្រេកឃ្លានយ៉ាងខ្លាំង និងបានខកចិត្ត។ ពួកគេជាច្រើននាក់បានស្លាប់។

ខ្ញុំបានជួបប្រទះទុក្ខព្រួយ និងវេទនា ដំព្រាលជ្រៅបំផុត នូវការបាត់បង់ប្រទេស និងមនុស្សជាទីស្រឡាញ់របស់ខ្ញុំ។ ខ្ញុំបានយំ ស្រែកយ៉ាងខ្លាំង ដែលចេញពីសេចក្ដីភ័យខ្លាច និងការលើចាប់ដំចំផេង ដែលខ្ញុំមានអារម្មណ៍ ខាងក្នុងចិត្ត និងបានសង្ឃឹមដល់សញ្ញានៃជំនួយខ្ញុំ។ ការតាំទ្រខាងផ្លូវចិត្ត ព្រលឹងវិញ្ញាណ ឬសំភារៈ ដំកូចគាតធ្វើមុខ មានតម្លៃប់លានដុល្លារ។

ខ្ញុំបានបន់ស្រន់ដល់ព្រះទាំងអស់ វិញ្ញាណទាំងអស់ ឲ្យជួយខ្ញុំគេចផុតពីសេចក្ដីន្ធត់ ដែលបានលងខ្ញុំ។

ខ្ញុំបានមកដល់សហរដ្ឋ ក្នុងខែកញ្ញា 1980 ក្នុងក្រុង Eugene រដ្ឋ Oregon និងបន្ទាប់មកទៀត ក៏បានផ្លាស់ទៅរដ្ឋ Minnesota ក្នុងខែធ្នូ 1980។ ខ្ញុំបាននទទួលបរិញ្ញាប័ត្រខាងសិល្បៈ ចេញពីសាកលវិទ្យាល័យ Metropolitan រដ្ឋ ក្នុងរដ្ឋ Minnesota នៅឆ្នាំ 1991។ ខ្ញុំបានក្លាយជាជំនួយយ៉ាងខ្លាំង ក្នុងការតំណាងឲ្យស្រ្តីខ្មែររបស់ខ្ញុំ និងបានធ្វើជាអ្នកដឹកនាំសហគមន៍ម្នាក់ ព្រមទាំងបានចូលប្រឡូកយ៉ាង សកម្ម នៅក្នុងអង្គការខ្មែរគ្មានកម្រៃជាច្រើន។

ខ្ញុំបានក្លាយជាអនុស្ថាបនិក នៃនិស្សិតខ្មែរនៅរដ្ឋ Minnesota និងជាស្ថាបនិកនៃសមាគមនៅរដ្ឋ Minnesota (UCAM)។ ខ្ញុំបានបំរើ ការងារជានាយកប្រតិបត្តិម្នាក់ ចាប់តាំងពីខែវិច្ឆិកា 1990 មក នៅពេលអ្នកកាន់តំណែងមុនខ្ញុំ ឈ្មោះមេង គ្រុយ អ៊ុង បានលាលែងតំណែង ដោយព្រោះជំងឺ ដែលបានទទួលមរណភាពមួយឆ្នាំក្រោយមក។

កំណាព្យមួយរបស់គាត់ ដែលមានន័យថា "បានទុកម្ដាយឲ្យនៅចាំយាមក្រុង" បានញ៉ាំងចិត្តខ្ញុំ ហើយខ្ញុំក៏បានប្ដេជ្ញាខ្លួនខ្ញុំ ឲ្យបានក្លាយជាមនុស្សគំរូម្នាក់ ចំពោះប្រទេសរបស់ខ្ញុំ ប្រជាជនរបស់ខ្ញុំ; ប្រហោជន៍ដើម្បីសង្ឃាតឲ្យក្លាយជាកូន ខ្មែរដ៏ល្អ ដើម្បីតបស្នងចំពោះការអង្វរករនៃម្ដាយគ្រប់ៗរូប សំរាប់ជាតិរបស់ខ្ញុំ។

French forced Hmong to pave the Road. They Murdered the French couple that came to govern Hmong.

diasporas like water

By Bryan Thao Worra

Winding through the course of our lives,
Memories like so many fish of war and loss,
Love and family.

Time takes its toll, ruthless, unrelenting.
The factory floor, the classroom so rarely
Requires an understanding of the distance

Between Saigon and Vientiane,
Long Cheng or Dien Bien Phu,
Let alone a high school horror story
In 1970s Phnom Penh.

Our ancestors would weep at half of
What we've forgotten already.

Our parents just want to eat one thing
That reminds them of the old country.
In the classrooms, their children hide their lunch
From prying peers who've no appreciation

For nuoc mam, padaek, or purple sticky rice.
The other day, a man came by who knew
Where we were from, for once.

Tried to say, "We're not so different,
Between the Mekong and the Mississippi,
10,000 lakes, and as many stories."

I want to be polite, accept that bridge,
Sturdy as the 35, but 45 years later
Our shared story can't be condensed

Into a made-for-TV mini-series,
Roots tangled, filtering, growing
Beneath a cold Northern Star

More than bamboo amid the pines,
The oaks, whatever it takes to rebuild.

I gather my fishing pole, a cassette recorder,
My family for a weekend away from it all.
Maybe the water will cleanse us,
Maybe the stories will return,

Sometimes a trickle. Sometimes a flood.

Nouth is from the countryside village of Ban Phon in Phon Hong district of Vientiane Province, Laos. She was a farm girl who knew the art of bamboo handicraft; quick on her feet and witty in the face of pressure. Nouth met Phanh, a senior royal army lieutenant from the city of Vientiane. They married and raised seven children. Nouth was 26 years old when the conflict ended in 1975. Phanh was a political prisoner for almost 10 years before Nouth would work up the courage to petition for his release.

Image courtesy of Nouth Phaengdara

S IS FOR SAMANA

ส. ສຳມະນາ

Nouth Phaengdara, 68
Minneapolis, MN

First, they took our men. My husband was a political prisoner before they forced him in samana labor camp. It was already 1984. I was 8-months pregnant with my daughter Chanida. My mother and I were raising all five children with the village aunties on our own. It took a toll on me. So I took a long bus ride to the samana labor camp. I asked the prison guards if I could visit my husband because I was going to go into labor soon. They told me if I brought all of my children with me to visit him, they would eventually let him go.

But when we entered the labor camp, we couldn't leave.

After the Americans left us, Laos wasn't the same. We had nothing. We were so poor. We had to give everything up. I was lucky to even have two pairs of clothes to wear and all of my children used the same cloth diaper to rewash over and over. In samana, we built homes and harvested the rice fields, grew vegetables, and raised chickens — just to feed everything to ai nong communists. To this day, I have a special appreciation for water buffalos because they made us till the soil with our bare hands and feet like animals. There was never enough food to feed everyone, so we portioned what we had to give to our family and friends.

I remember when my 2 year old son became really sick and we didn't know what to do. An army medic gave him penicillin. My frail boy held his neck, his face turned pale and he couldn't breathe. I kept shaking him and breathing into his mouth. I never cried so hard in my life. I went crazy after that. Neither of us knew he would be allergic. He died by the river. Anyone who spoke up about it would disappear overnight.

I want to forget that time in our lives. The time in samana aren't memories I want to recover. That's how I survived and kept my children alive. Before I remember, I also have to forget. I would stand in the rice fields and see the beauty in the landscape first, the lush forests and flowing Mekong.

ນຸດ ແພງດາລາ, ອາຍຸ **68** ປີ
Minneapolis

ນຸດ ເຕີບໃຫຍ່ຢູ່ຊຸບບະນິດທີ່ ບ້ານໂພນ, ເມືອງໂພນໂຮງ ແຂວງວຽງຈັນ, ບາງເປັນຊາວໄຮ່ຊາວນາທີ່ຮູ້ຈັກການສາບເປັນຢ່າງດີ. ນຸດໄດ້ພິບກັບສາມິຂອງລາວທີ່ເປັນ ພິນໂທໃນບະຄອບທູ່ວງວຽງຈັນ, ມີບານ ອ່າ ພັນ, ທັງສອງໄດ້ແຕ່ງງານ ແລະ ມີລູກນຳກັນ 7 ຄົນ, ນຸດໄດ້ອາຍຸ 26 ປີຕອບທີ່ບ້ານເມືອງກຳລັງ ທຸຍ້ຍຍາກ ໃນປີ1975. ພັນ, ສາມິຂອງນຸດໄດ້ຖຶກຈຳຄຸກເກືອບ 10 ປີ ກ່ອນທີ່ນຸດໄດ້ກ້າຮ້ອງຂໍ ເພື່ອໃຫ້ສາມິ ຂອງລາວຖຶກປ່ອຍຕິວ.

ສາມິຂອງຂ້າພະເຈົ້າເປັນນັກໂທດທາງການເມືອງກ່ອນທີ່ຈະຖຶກສົ່ງໄປສຳມະນາໃນປີ 1984. ຕອບນັ້ນຂ້າ ພະເຈົ້າກຶພາລູກສາວຊື່ ຈັນນິດາ ໄດ້ 8 ເດືອນ. ແມ່ ແລະ ຂ້າພະເຈົ້າ ຮັບພາລະລ້ງງລູກເອງ ແລະ ໄດ້ຮັບ ການຊ່ວຍເຫຼືອ ຂອງ ປ້າ, ນ້າ, ອາແຖວນັ້ນ. ກ່ອນທີ່ຈະເກິດລູກຂ້າພະເຈົ້າມີຈຸດປະສິງ

ຢາກໄປປາມສາມິ ຢູ່ສູບສຳມະບາ. ເຈົ້າໜ້າທີ່ກໍໄດ້ເວົ້າວ່າ, ຖ້າຂ້ອຍເອົາລູກທຸກຄົນໄປປາມບໍ່ຳ, ບາງທີສາມິຂ້ອຍອາດຖືກປ່ອຍຕົວ.

ແຕ່ໃນຄວາມເປັນຈິງ, ເວລາທີ່ເຂົ້າໄປແລ້ວ ເຂົາເຈົ້າບໍ່ປ່ອຍໃຫ້ພວກເຮົາອອກມາເລີຍ.

ພາຍຫຼັງທີ່ສະທະລັດອາເມລິກາໄດ້ຕອບໂຕອອກຈາກ ສປປ ລາວ, ທຸກສິ່ງທຸກຢ່າງກໍປ່ຽນໄປ. ພວກເຮົາ ຕົກທຸກໄດ້ຍາກທຽນ, ຂ້າພະເຈົ້າບໍ່ມີຫຍັງຕິດຕົວເລີຍ, ມີພຽງແຕ່ເຄື່ອງນຸ່ງຄາຕິງ, ລູກຂອງຂ້າພະເຈົ້າກໍໃສ່ ແຕ່ຜ້າອ້ອມເກົ່າທີ່ຊຸກ ແລະ ໃສ່ກັບໄປກັບມາ. ຢູ່ສຳມະບາ, ພວກເຮົາເຮັດໜົດທຸກຢ່າງທັ້ງ ປຸກເຮືອນ, ເກັບກູ່ວເຂົ້າ, ປຸກຜັກ, ລ້ຽງໄກ່, ເຮັດທຸກຢ່າງເພື່ອລ້ຽງອ້າຍບ້ອງຄອມມຸນິດ; ຍ້ອນແນວນັ້ນ, ຂ້າພະເຈົ້າ ຈຶ່ງຮູ້ ຄຸນຄ່າຂອງຄວາຍຫຼາຍເພາະພວກເຮົາຕ້ອງພູບຄິບດ້ວຍການໃຊ້ມີ ແລະ ຄົບຄັ່ງປາບພວກເຮົາເປັນ ໂຕ ສັດ. ອາຫານທີ່ພວກເຮົາໄດ້ກໍບໍ່ພຽງພໍ, ທຸກສິ່ງທີ່ໄດ້ຕ້ອງແບ່ງເພື່ອໃຫ້ພໍກັບກິນ.

ຂ້າພະເຈົ້າຍັງຈື່ໄດ້ດີ, ຕອນລູກຊາຍບໍ່ສະບາຍ ແລະ ລົ້ມປ່ວຍລົງ, ທະຫານໄດ້ເອົາຢາຕ້ານເຊື້ອໃຫ້ ລາວກິນ ແຕ່ຫຼັງຈາກນັ້ນຕົບໂຕ ແລະ ໜ້າຕາລາວກໍເລີ່ມຈິດ ແລ້ວລາວກໍ່ຫາຍໃຈບໍ່ອອກ. ຂ້າພະເຈົ້າພະຍາຍາມປຸກ ແລະ ເປົ່າລົມໃສ່ປາກເພື່ອໃຫ້ລາວຫາຍໃຈແຕ່ກໍບໍ່ເປັນຜົນ. ບໍ່ມີໃຜຮູ້ເລີຍວ່າລູກຂອງ ຂ້າພະເຈົ້າແພ້ຢາ, ລູກ ຂອງຂ້າພະເຈົ້າໜິດລົມຫາຍໃຈຢູ່ແກວແຄມບໍ່ຳ, ຂ້າພະເຈົ້າຮ້ອງໃຫ້ປາບຄິບບ້າໜັ້ງ ຈາກທີ່ສູບເສຍລູກ. ໃຜ ກໍ່ຢ່າທີ່ເວົ້າກໍ່ວອກັບເລື່ອງນີ້ກໍ່ຈະຫາຍສາບສູບໃນທັນທີ.

ຂ້າພະເຈົ້າພະຍາຍາມທີ່ສຸດທີ່ຈະລືມເຫດການຕ່າງໆທີ່ເກີດຂຶ້ນຢູ່ສຳມະບາ ເພື່ອຮັກສາຊີວິດຂອງລູກໆຂ້າ ພະເຈົ້າ. ກ່ອນທີ່ຈະຈື່, ຂ້າພະເຈົ້າຈຳຕ້ອງລືມ. ສິ່ງທີ່ຂ້າພະເຈົ້າເຮັດໄດ້ເພື່ອລືມມີພຽງແຕ່ຍືນກາງທົ່ງນາ ແລະ ຊືມຄວາມງາມຂອງຮັດສະນິຍະ ພາບ, ປ່າໄມ້ ແລະ ນ້ຳຂອງ.

"When water buffaloes fight,
it is the grass that suffers."

Lao Proverb

LOVE IS AN ETERNAL LESSON

Tình thương là bài học vĩnh viễn

Dương Như Hà, 75
Saint Paul

I was born in 1943 at Ninh Binh province in the Northern part of Vietnam into a family with generations of prosperity, and my father was a teacher in a French school. The 1945 famine was the earliest memory I had about the war, at the age of three. I recall my mother cooking a huge amount of rice mixed with bran, but it was still not sufficient to feed the starving groups of people who sometimes poured into my house garden to look for food. The famine that year was a result of the heartless Japanese soldiers who forced the Việt to pull up all the ripe rice flowers and dump into the sea in order to grow jute, a kind of raw material to serve the war.

My next memory was that of the war between the Viet Minh and the French. Viet Minh's strategy at the time forced the Northern Việt to constantly evacuate from their current dwellings. During this time, my father continued his mission as an educator, teaching people he met on the way. Even though he was disconnected from his French school where he received his salary, my family was still strongly supported by the local people because the Northern Việt at the time highly respected teachers. In 1954, my mother brought all of her children to relocate in the South using my father's retirement income left for her after he passed away.

I absorbed the education of the South Regime in Saigon. At that time, the philosophy taught in school opened students up to the freedom of knowledge. Their mindset was not restrained by any one regimen. In my twenties, I became a high school math teacher while also pursuing my passion in the arts. I was also in the first cohort of the renowned Indochina Artistic College.

I joined the South Việt army in the special task force as a second lieutenant. I completed my military career in three years, after leaving behind my left arm at Tram Bridge at the end of the Ho Chi Minh Trail.

After I was discharged from the army, I got married and lived a peaceful, wealthy life. When the Communists occupied the South of Vietnam in 1975, it was very clear to me that I could not let my family live under that regime. At that time, I already had five children and had to take on many different businesses

to earn enough income to provide for the family, but none of these jobs lasted long under the interference of the local government. After eight failed attempts to escape the country by boat, my two sons and I finally arrived in the Philippines.

Thinking that all the hardship had passed, my sons and I were then constantly excluded from the list of political refugees to immigrate into the US, even though I exceeded the requirements set forth by the US government. The price I paid for my belief in justice and fairness, and my determination to not nurture corruption, was 11 years being stuck at Palawan refugee camps in the Philippines.

I arrived in the US in 2000 and adapted to the new life in the US with all of my strength, the inner strength of a loving father, and the steadfast spirit of a commander in the past battlefield. My whole family is now united in their new home country, but life has continued with both successes and challenges. My wife and I are now grandparents of five beautiful grandchildren.

Reflecting on my life so far, I affirm that all are blessings. The love I receive from God has always been with me, silent but sturdy. The true love that is transferred from one to another can be so strong and contain limitless transformative power. My life has always been carried by these waves of love so I can now pass them on to the next generation, starting right here in Minnesota.

————

Dương Như Hà, 75
Saint Paul

Tôi sinh năm 1943 tại tỉnh Ninh Bình, Miền Bắc Việt Nam, trong một gia đình nhiều đời thịnh vượng và cha tôi là một thầy giáo trường Pháp. Nạn đói năm 1945 là kí ức chiến tranh sớm nhất của tôi, khi ấy mới chỉ hơn ba tuổi. Tôi vẫn nhớ hình ảnh mẹ mình nấu thật nhiều cơm độn với cám mà vẫn không đủ để phân phát cho đoàn người đói mỗi sáng, có lúc tràn vào đến sân nhà tôi để kiếm lương thực. Năm đó, quân đội Nhật tàn ác đã bắt người dân Việt nhổ hết lúa đang trổ đòng để trồng đay-loại cây nguyên liệu phục vụ chiến tranh.

Kí ức kế tiếp của tôi là cuộc chiến giữa Việt Minh với Pháp. Chiến lược của Việt Minh thời bấy giờ buộc người dân Bắc Việt phải liên tục sơ tán khỏi nơi họ đang định cư. Cha tôi trong thời gian này vẫn tiếp tục nhiệm vụ của một vị giáo chức: đi đến đâu dạy học đến đó. Dù mất liên lạc với trường Pháp nơi ông đang nhận nguồn lương, gia đình tôi vẫn nhận được nhiều sự giúp đỡ vì thời bấy giờ người dân Bắc Việt hết

sức kính trọng nghề giáo. Năm 1954, với số tiền lương hưu của cha tôi để lại sau khi qua đời, mẹ tôi mang gia đình di cư vào Nam.

Tôi hàm thụ nền giáo dục dưới thời Việt Nam Cộng Hoà tại Sài Gòn. Kiến thức triết học mở ra cho người dân sự tự do hiểu biết, tư tưởng họ không bị giới hạn bởi bất cứ chế độ độc tôn nào. Những năm ngoài hai mươi tuổi, tôi trở thành thầy giáo dạy toán bậc trung học, đồng thời theo đuổi đam mê mỹ thuật và trở thành một trong những người thuộc thế hệ đầu tiên của trường cao đẳng mỹ thuật Đông Dương sau này.

Tôi nhập ngũ vào trường Sỹ quan Việt Nam Cộng Hoà và trở thành Biệt động quân với quân hàm Thiếu Úy. Sau ba năm, tôi hoàn thành cuộc đời chiến binh của mình, để lại cánh tay trái tại Cầu Tràm cuối đường mòn Hồ Chí Minh.

Sau khi giải ngũ, tôi lập gia đình và sống một cuộc sống yên ấm, khá giả. Khi Việt Cộng chiếm miền Nam năm 1975, tôi biết rõ là không thể để gia đình mình sống dưới chế độ cộng sản và ấp ủ quyết tâm ra đi. Lúc này, tôi đã có năm người con, trải qua rất nhiều công việc kinh doanh để nuôi sống gia đình nhưng chẳng công việc nào kéo dài được lâu dưới sự sách nhiễu của chính quyền địa phương. Sau tám lần vượt biên thất bại, tôi cùng hai người con trai đến được Philippin.

Những tưởng sóng gió đã qua đi, không ngờ tôi cùng hai con trai liên tục bị loại khỏi danh sách tị nạn chính trị mặc dù hội tụ trên mức đầy đủ những yêu cầu của chính phủ Mỹ. Cái giá của sự tin tưởng vào lẽ công bằng, nhất quyết không tiếp tay nuôi dưỡng tham nhũng là 11 năm trời kẹt lại trại tị nạn Palawan, Philippin.

Tôi đến Mỹ năm 2000 và hoà nhập vào cuộc sống tại đây với tất cả nội lực của một người cha cùng tinh thần kiên cường của người chỉ huy nơi chiến trường năm xưa. Cả gia đình tôi nay đã đoàn tụ trên quê hương mới, cuộc sống tiếp diễn với nhiều thành công và thách đố. Vợ chồng tôi nay đã trở thành ông bà của năm đứa cháu xinh xắn.

Nhìn lại cuộc đời mình, tôi có thể khẳng định: " Tất Cả Là Hồng n". Nguồn Tình Yêu tôi nhận được từ Thiên Chúa luôn hiện diện, thầm lặng nhưng mãnh liệt. Tình yêu chân thật truyền từ người này đến người kia vô cùng mạnh mẽ và mang sức biến đổi vô biên. Cả cuộc đời, tôi vẫn luôn được dìu đi bởi những cơn sóng tình yêu đó để rồi đến lượt mình truyền lại cho thế hệ sau, khởi đi từ Minnesota này.

Image courtesy of Dương Như Hà,

Image by Son Tran

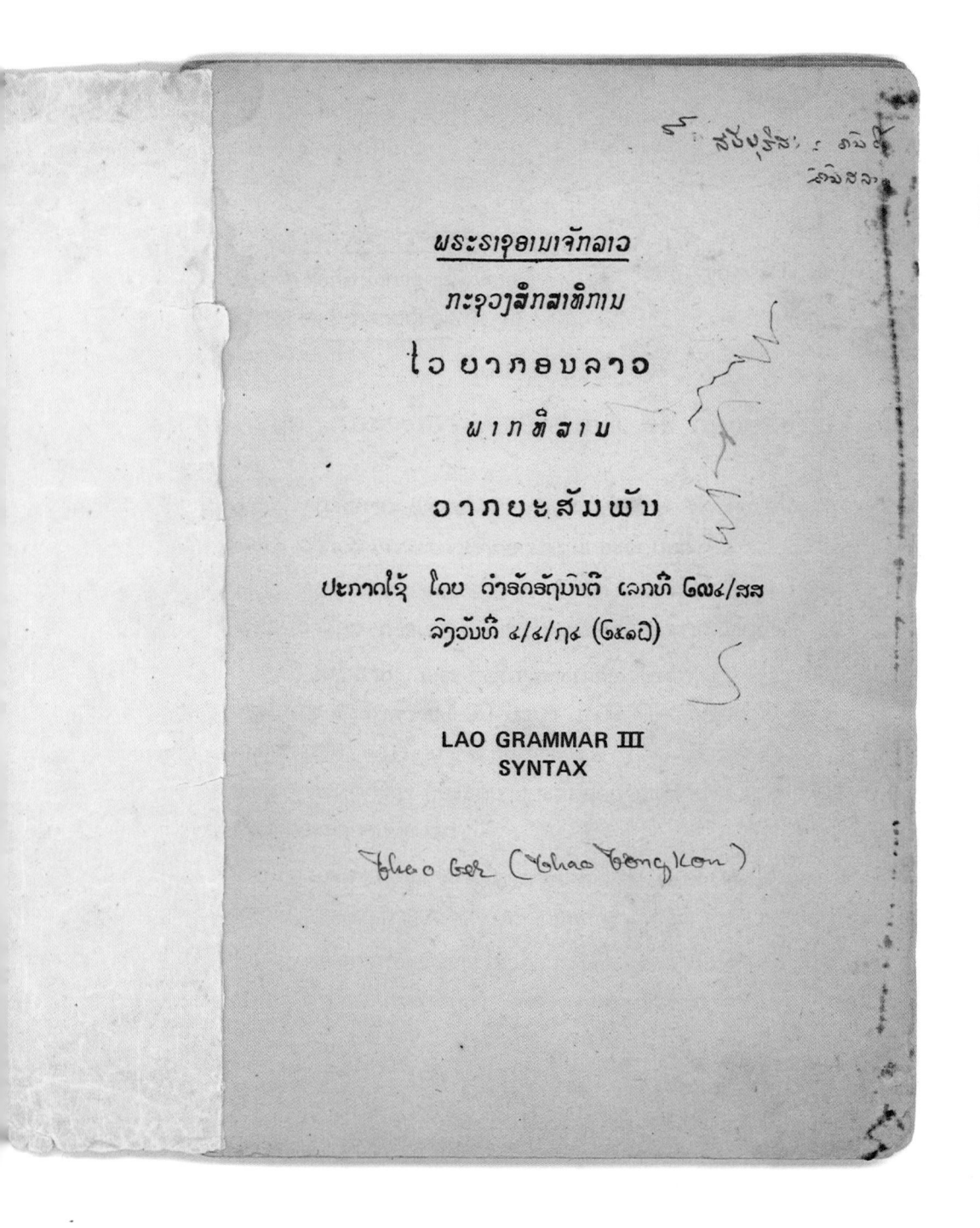

ພຣະຣາຊອານາຈັກລາວ

ກະຊວງສຶກສາທິການ

ໄວ ຍາກອນລາວ

ພາກທີສາມ

ວາກຍະສັມພັນ

ປະກາດໃຊ້ ໂດຍ ຄຳຮັດຮັຖມິນຕີ ເລກທີ ໑໘໔/ສສ
ລົງວັນທີ ໔/໔/໗໔ (໑໙໑໓)

LAO GRAMMAR III
SYNTAX

Thao Ger (Thao Tong Kou)

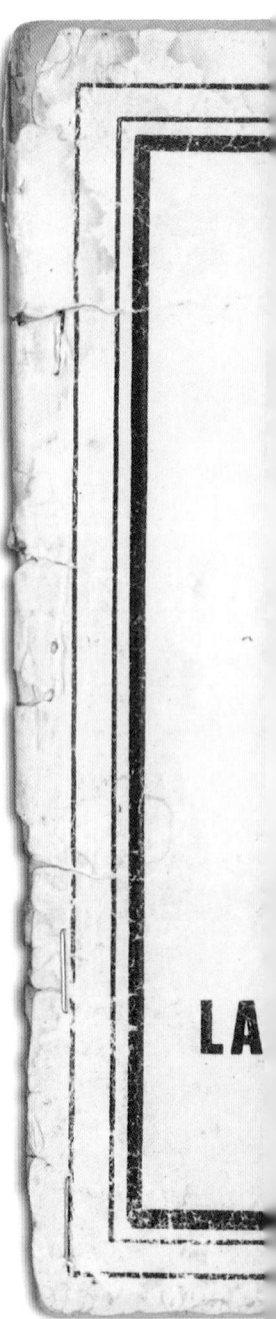

MY NAME IS NTXAWG

Kuv Lub Npe Hu Ua Ntxawg

Tong Kou Thao, 58
Saint Paul

My given name growing up is Ger (Ntxawg). If you are the last born in your family, Hmong people would often name you Ger or Yer. Even when I went to school in Laos, the Lao teachers and other students called me bakla meaning baby boy in Lao. I was born May 15, 1960 but when we arrived in the United States my birthday was changed to June 15, 1961. My home village is Phong Sai in Vang Vieng, a small town near Vientiane. One of my fondest childhood memories was with my father. We sat around the house and shared riddles. Now, I tell those same riddles to my children.

My oldest brother, Nhia Chia, taught me how to read and write in Lao and French. Before I was old enough to go to school, I looked forward to him coming home from school to teach me what he learned. Growing up I was a naughty kid. It's silly to think about, but yeah, I was lazy. As a young boy, maybe 5 or 6 years old, I hated doing chores. My parents would wake me up at dawn to go to the gardens. We had to get there early so that it was cool enough to get anything done before the heat arrived. Reluctantly, I went with them because I didn't want to be left home alone, but I wanted to stay back so I could read. Eventually, it became easier to help with gardening. Once, I woke up before my parents and beat them to the gardens. By the time they arrived, I had already hunted squirrels with my crossbow and roasted them for breakfast.

I helped with gardening until 1968, when I started year one of school. While my brothers went on to join Vang Pao's CIA forces, I continued with school up until lycee. In 1975, I became a student teacher and taught alongside the professors. In 1979, I obtained my teaching diploma. I loved my teaching job but it was cut short in 1980. I never wanted to leave Laos. That was my home. I only left because my older brother, Chia Vang, and mom convinced me to go to the gardens to ua neeb. I'll never forget that morning. When I arrived at the gardens, they told me we were running away. I didn't have a choice! We slashed and burned our gardens and then ran into the jungles. It took us another year to finally make it to the Mekong.

I took up teaching again in Vinai refugee camp. I taught Thai and math, my favorite subject. By 1989, I was training other people to become teachers. In 1993, we left Vinai for Phanat Nikhom and on June 2, 1994, my mom, wife, five kids and I arrived in Minnesota. I obtained my GED within the first year and would have gone on to get my teaching license to teach ELL, but my wife convinced me to enter the workforce. I worked at a candy factory until I had a stroke in 2007. Every so often I would run into former students who are now interpreters for me during hospital check-ups. They would say "Mr. Thao, thank you for teaching me. I have this job because you inspired me." It's bittersweet.

My eldest son just obtained his masters degree and wants to become a school principal. I laugh because he wants to be a teacher too! I keep telling him that being a school principal is going to be a tough job, but as long as he's happy he should keep at it. I want my children to remember to never give up on their dreams. Whatever they want to do in life, they should do it to their fullest potential. I never obtained any degrees in America, but I'm proud that my children did.

Ntooj Kub Thoj, 58
Saint Paul

Luj hlub lug lub npe kws muab rua kuv yog Ntxawg. Yog koj yog tus yug tom kawg, Hmoob feem ntau yuav muab koj lub npe tis hu Ntxawg los sis Ntxawm. Thaum kuv moog kawm ntawv nyob huv Nplog teb, cov xib fwb Nplog hab cov tub ntxhais kawm yeej muab kuv hu ua bakla, nws txhais has tas "me ab tub" nyob rua lus Nplog. Kuv yug rua lub 5 hlis ntuj hnub tim 15, xyoo 1960, taab sis thaum peb tuaj txug teb chaws Meskas, kuv lub hnub nyoog raug hloov moog ua lub 6 hli hnub tim 15, xyoo 1961 lawm. Kuv lub zej zog hu ua Phong Sai nyob lub nroog Vang Vieng, yog ib lub zog miv miv npuab lub nroog Vientiane. Ib lub sij hawm kws kuv ncu tshaaj plawg thaum kuv tseem miv, yog thaum kuv nrug kuv txiv. Ib tau zaum ncig peb lub tsev hab thaam paaj lug ua ke. Zag nuav, kuv ho yog tug lug pav kuv txiv ib cov paaj lug nuav rua kuv cov miv nyuag.

Kuv tug tij laug hlub tshaaj nyob rua huv peb tsev neeg, lub npe hu ua Nyaj Nchaiv, nws tau qha kuv nyeem hab sau ntawv Nplog hab Fabkis. Ua ntej thaum kuv tseem tsis tau moog kawm ntawv, kuv tsuas nyob tsev ntsa ntsoov thaum nwg lug tom tsev kawm ntawv lug, es lug qha kuv txug cov kws nwg tau kawm. Luj hlub lug kuv yog ib tug miv nyuag kws khib lwb heev. Xaav txug mas yeej txaus luag kawg hab, taab sis muab has lug teg kuv yog ib tug neeg tub nkeeg kawg. Vim kuv yog ib tug miv nyuag tub, muaj 5 los sis 6 xyoo xwb, kuv tsis nyam ua hauj lwm kag le. Thaum hnub tawm kag xwb tes kuv nam hab kuv txiv yeej tsaa kuv sawv es peb moog tom teb. Peb yuav tsum tau moog kom ntxuv thaum nwg tseem txag, es peb txhaj le ua tau teb ntau ua ntej tshaav ntuj yuav kub. Kuv tsuas laam moog nrug puab lawm xwb vim kuv tsis xaav nyob tsev tuab leeg, taab sis kuv ho xaav nyob tsev vim kuv xaav nyeem ntawv. Tsis ntev xwb, moog ua teb kuj pib yooj yim zog lawm. Muaj ib zag, kuv tau sawv ua ntej kuv nam hab kuv txiv ob tug, teg kuv ca le moog tom teb tuab leeg ua ntej. Thaum kuv nam hab kuv txiv ob tug tuaj txug pem teb teg, kuv twb nqaa kuv rab neev moog tua tau nas coj lug ci rua peb noj tshais lawm.

Kuv tau paab ua peb dlaim teb txug ntua xyoo 1968, thaum kws kuv tau moog pib kawm ntawv xyoo ib rua pem tsev kawm ntawv. Kuv cov tij laug tau moog ua Nai Phoo Vaaj Pov cov tub rog CIA (Central Intelligence Agency) lawm. Hos kuv teg tau kawm ntxiv txug ntua lycee. Nyob rua xyoo 1975, kuv tau rais lug ua ib tug tub kawm ua paab qha ntawv nrug rua cov xib fwb. Nyob rua xyoo 1979, kuv kuj tau kawm tav kuv dlaim Diploma lug ua ib tug xib fwb qha ntawv. Kuv nyam kuv txuj hauj lwm qha ntawv kawg, taab sis nyob rua xyoo 1980 kuv tau muab tso tseg lawm. Kuv ib txwm yeej tsis xaav ncaim lub teb chaws Nplog kag le. Nws yog kuv lub tsev. Kuv tsuas laam ua ib sab ncaim vim kuv tug tij laug, Txaj Vaas, hab kuv nam ob tug tau has kom kuv nrug nkawv moog ua neeb tom teb. Kuv yeej yuav tsis nov qaab hnub sawv ntxuv hov kag le. Thaum peb moog txug tom teb, ob tug ca le has rua kuv has tas peb yuav tsiv. Kuv tsis muaj hauv kev lawm. Peb tau hlais hab hlawv peb cov teb, teg peb ca le tsiv rua tom haav zoov lawm. Peb twb tsiv tau ib lub xyoos dlam peb maam le lug txug tug dlej Naab Khoom.

Kuv rov qaab pib qha ntawv dlua rua huv lub Yeej Thoj Nam Tawg Rog Vib Nais. Kuv qha lug Thaib hab leb, uas yog qhov nyam tshaaj. Txug ntua xyoo 1989, kuv twb tau lug cob qha tib neeg lug ua xib fwb qha ntawv. Nyob rua xyoo 1993, peb tau ncaim Vib Nais moog rua lub zog Phanat Nikhom, teg nyob rua lub 6 hli ntuj hnub tim 2, xyoo 1994, kuv nam, kuv tug quag puj, nrug rua kuv tsib tug miv nyuag hab kuv, peb tau tuaj txug lub xeev Minnesota. Kuv tau moog kawm tav kuv dlaim GED (General Educational Development) thawj xyoo kws peb tuaj txug. Kuv twb xaav tas yuav mus kawm ntxiv kom tau kuv dlaim license qha ntawv ELL (English Language Learner), taab sis kuv tug quag puj tau has kom kuv moog ua hauj lwm lwm yaam. Kuv txhaj tau moog ua hauj lwm nyob rua ib lub hoob kas kws ua qhob noom, txug ntua thaum xyoo 2007 kws kuv tau mob stroke. Tej thaum kws kuv moog tom hoos maum, kuv kuj moog ntsib ncaaj kuv cov tub ntxhais kawm, uas taam sim nuav lug yog tug txhais lug rua kuv. Puab has tas " Xib fwb Thoj, ua tsaug qhov kws koj qha ntawv rua kuv. Kuv tau txuj hauj lwm nuav los twb vim yog muaj koj ua ib tug qauv zoo rua kuv." Qhov nuav, nws qaab zib taab sis kuj ab kawg hab.

Kuv tug tub hlub kag nyaav kawm tav nwg dlaim masters degree. Nws xaav lug ua ib tug thawj tswj huv tsev kawm ntawv. Kuv tuaj dlaab ros vim nws kuj xaav lug ua ib tug xib fwb hab! Kuv yeej qha nwg taag zug has tas ua ib tug thawj tswj huv tsev kawm ntawv nwg yuav nyuab, taab sis tsuav yog nwg nyam hab zoo sab xwb teg kaav tsij ua tag. Kuv xaav kom kuv cov miv nyuag tsis txhob muab puab tej kev npau suav tso tseg. Yaam twg kws puab xaav ua nyob rua huv puab lub neej, puab yuav tsum sib zug peem ua moog kom kawg. Nyob rua huv kuv lub neej kuv yeej tsis tau ib dlaim degree nyob rua lub teb chaws Meskas nuav, taab sis kuv zoo sab has tas kuv cov miv nyuag twb tau lawm.

Image courtesy of Bounlieng Daoheuang

THE WAR IS OVER, DROP YOUR GUNS

ສົງຄາມໄດ້ຈົບລົງແລ້ວ, ອາງປືນລົງ

Bounlieng Daoheuang, 77
Minneapolis

Major Bounlieng was born in Savannakhet, Laos. He joined the Royal Lao Army as a teenager, doing the military's finances before being recruited by the CIA to provide intelligence in their operations during Operation Barrel Roll. He lives in Minneapolis with his wife, Khanthong Daoheuang. This is their exchange.

"After the French left, I was just finishing up high school in Savannakhet and got into the army right away. They sent me to Xieng Khouang and Long Cheng for long periods of time."

"He was gone all the time. I raised three children on my own."

"When we first met, it was 1965 in Vientiane. I asked her parents if I could marry her right away. I paid around 250,00 Kip for the wedding."

"I don't remember any of this well. He has better memory than me. And he's the one with the physical disabilities."

"Our house was in Dongpalane near the old theater. They ransacked our house, took our money and burned it. We had nothing left."

"Ah yes, I remember that."

"John* who was leading the CIA asked me to bring him

intel back to basecamp, with the promise that our safety to America was ensured."

"You did it for free."

"I did it for one year. I wanted to make sure we got to America alive. But after the Americans left, they said to us that the war was over and to drop our guns. I was put in the Sepon labor camp where the ethnic Ga were guards. They would take our knives away every night. If there were any complaints, people disappeared the next morning."

"He was always sick, in and out of the hospital."

"It was September of 1978 when we arrived in Minneapolis. We were one of seven Lao families who boarded the same plane. I remember my skin tightening up from the cold wind. It was boring, often lonely. Learning how to use the bath faucet was challenging. The first donation we got from our sponsor was an old couch. It had a strong dog stench to it. But we slept on it anyway."

———

ບຸນລ່ຽງ ດາວເຮືອງ, ອາຍຸ **77** ປີ
Minneapolis

ພັນຕີ ບຸນລ່ຽງ ກຳເນີດຢູ່ແຂວງສະຫວັນນະເຂດ, ແລະ ເຂົ້າສັງກັດເປັນທະຫານ ທີ່ທະຫານພະທາລຸອາບາ ຈັກລາວ ຕອນຍັງໜຸ່ມນ້ອຍ ແລະ ໄດ້ຮັບພ້າທີ່ເປັນພະນັກງານບັນຊີ ກ່ອນທີ່ຈະຖືກທາບທາມ ໂດຍ CIA ເພື່ອເຂົ້າຮ່ວມເຮັດວຽກໃນໄລຍະ Operation Barrel Roll ຫຼື ໜ່ວຍງານລັບ. ປະຈຸບັນ, ທ່ານ ພັນຕີ ອາໄສຢູ່ເມືອງມີນີເອັບໂປລີດ ກັບ ພັນລະຍາຂອງເພິ່ນ, ທ່ານ ບາງ ຂັນທອງ ດາວເຮືອງ.

"ພາຍຫຼັງທີ່ສະທະພານຝຣັ່ງໄດ້ຖອນກຳລັງ, ຂ້າພະເຈົ້າເອງພອມ ກຳລັງຈະຈົບມັດທະຍົມຕອນປາຍຢູ່ ແຂວງສະຫວັນນະເຂດ ແລະ ເຂົ້າສັງກັດເປັນທະຫານທັນທີ. ເຂົາເຈົ້າໄດ້ສົ່ງຂ້າພະເຈົ້າໄປແຂວງຊຽງຂວາງ ແລະ ລ່ອງແຈ້ງເປັນເວລາດົນສົມຄວນ."

"ລາວບໍ່ໄດ້ຢູ່ບຳຄອບຖືເປັນເວລາດົນ, ສ່ວນຂ້ອຍເອງກໍ່ຕ້ອງແບກຮັບພາລະລ້ຽງ ດູ ແລະ ເບິ່ງແຍງລູກໆ ຕາມລຳພັງ."

"ພອກເຮົາພົບກັນຄັ້ງທຳອິດແມ່ນໄລຍະປີ 1965 ຢູ່ນະຄອນຫຼວງວຽງຈັນ. ຂ້າພະເຈົ້າເອງໄດ້ຂໍແຕ່ງພັນລະຍາ ບຳໜ່ແມ່ຂອງເພິ່ນດ້ວຍເງິນຈຳຄອນ 250,000 ກີບເທົ່ານັ້ນ."

"ຂ້າພະເຈົ້າບໍ່ຈື່ເລື່ອງລາວຕ່າງໆປານໃດ, ສາມາດຈະຈື່ໄດ້ດີກ່ວາ ແລະ

ລາວເປັນຄົນເສຍອິງຄະ."

"ບ້ານຂອງພວກເຮົາຕັ້ງຢູ່ບ້ານຄົງປ່າລາບ, ໃກ້ກັບໂຮງຮຽນເກົ່າເກົ່າ. ເຮືອນຂອງພວກເຮົາຖືກຍິງປືນ, ເຂົາລັກ
ເອົາເຄື່ອນ ແລະ ຈຸດເຜົາເຮືອນ, ພວກເຮົາບໍ່ເຫຼືອຫຍັງເລີຍ."

"ໂອ, ຂ້ອຍຈົ່ໄດ້ແລ້ວ."

"ຈອນ*, ເປັນທ້ອງຫ້າທິມ CIA ແລະໄດ້ໃຫ້ຄຳໝັ້ນສັນຍາກັບຂ້າພະເຈົ້າວ່າ ຖ້າບຳສິ່ງເອົາຂໍ້ມູນ ໃຫ້ລາວຢູ່ຄ້າຍ,
ລາວຈະຊ່ວຍຂ້າພະເຈົ້າໃນການອົບພະຍົກໄປສະຫະລັດອາເມລິກາຢ່າງປອດໄພ."

"ເຈົ້າເຮັດວຽກໃຫ້ເຂົາເຈົ້າລາລ້າ."

"ຂ້າພະເຈົ້າເຮັດວຽກນັ້ນໄດ້ຫ້າງປີ, ຂ້າພະເຈົ້າເຮັດທຸກຢ່າງເພື່ອໃຫ້ໄດ້ຍົກຍ້າຍໄປສະຫະລັດອາເມລິ
ກາ. ແຕ່ພາຍຫຼັງທີ່ສະຫະລັດອາເມລິກາຖອນໂຕອອກ, ສິ່ງຄາມກໍ່ໄດ້ຍຸຕິລົງ ແລະ ເຂົາເຈົ້າກໍ່ໄດ້ບອກໃຫ້
ພວກເຮົາວາງປືນລົງ. ຫຼັງຈາກນັ້ນ, ຂ້າພະເຈົ້າເອງກໍ່ຖືກສັ່ງໄປຢູ່ຄ້າຍແຮງງານຢູ່ເຊໂປນ
ທີ່ຊົບເຜົ່າກໍ່ໄດ້ເຝົ້າຍາມ ຕະຫຼອດເວລາ ແລະ ຖ້າຜູ້ໃດຄິດຂືນ ຫຼື ຄິດຄ້ານໃດໆຈະຫາຍສາບສູນທັນທີ."

"ລາວມັກບໍ່ສະບາຍຕະຫຼອດ, ເຂົ້າອອກໂຮງໝໍຕະຫຼອດເລີຍ."

"ພວກເຮົາເປັນ 1 ໃນ 7 ຄອບຄົວ ທີ່ເດີນທາງຮອດເມືອງມິນິເອັບໂປລິດ ໄລຍະເຄືອນກັບຍາ
ປີ 1978. ຂ້າພະເຈົ້າຍັງຈົ່ໄດ້ດີວ່າ ຊ່ວງນັ້ນເປັນຊ່ວງທີ່ອາກາດໜາວຫຼາຍ ແລະ ຜົວໜັງແຫ້ງຕິງ.
ບັນຍາກາດນັ້ນເທງໆ ແລະ ໜ້າເບື່ອທີ່ສຸດ. ຮຽນໃຊ້ເຄື່ອງສຸກະພັນເປັນສິ່ງທີ່ຍາກທີ່ສຸດສຳລັບຂ້າພະເຈົ້າ
ໃນເວລານັ້ນ. ສິ່ງຂອງທຳຂິດທີ່ພວກເຮົາໄດ້ ຮັບຈາກການບໍລິຈາກກໍຄືໂຊຟາເກົ່າໆທີ່ມີກິ່ນແຮງຂອງໝາ,
ແຕ່ກໍ່ກາຍເປັນບ່ອນນອນທີ່ດີ ທີ່ສຸດຂອງພວກເຮົາໃນເວລານັ້ນ."

We are in the

By Narate Keys

ancestors making

We are ancestors in the making
Changing and adapting
We are SEAD that bloom
Years of budding

Await
Agate
Apart
Abundance

We are ancestors in the making
Connecting one person at a time
Community conversation
Taken place
Storytelling in discussion

To plant
To SEAD
That grown
Into adulthood

We are ancestors in the making
Chains of reactions
Chains of change
Change in you
Change in us.

We are
You are
Y.o.u. Are
Ancestry in the making...

CRIME. WANTING TO BE TOO FREE

THE PEOPLE'S MEDIC

ແพດຂອງປະຊາຊົນ

*Sun S., 64
Minneapolis

Sun was born in a forest in Attapeu when independence from the French Union occurred in 1954. He was a trained physician assistant in Laos before arriving in Minneapolis where he's currently a practicing nurse. He lives with his wife in the Twin Cities.

I grew up in Attapeu until 12-years-old and evacuated to Pakse to finish school when the war turned heavy. My earliest memory was raised around gunfire and family members dying from bombs and guns. In 1963 to 1964, I was in 5th grade when the war got even heavier.

When I was a little boy, there wasn't much to do. My village was impoverished. We didn't have running clean water, no working toilet. We didn't have flooring. Just dirt floor. It's where my parents dug a foxhole to crawl in when we were told to go hide for safety.

In 1968, the Pathet Lao began moving into our province. They evacuated only high school students in my village and district, to keep us away from the war zone. We went to live in a small dormitory in Pakse. We were separated from our parents, but they didn't want to interrupt our education while the fighting was still going on, so we stayed in Pakse even through the summers. I was there for three years. As teenagers, we couldn't think about what was happening around us and we were too busy to think about whether or not our families were alive. I had to focus on my studies and played guitar and soccer to pass time.

I went to medical school in Vientiane 1972 until 1976, to be a physician assistant. In October, 1976, the same time I graduated, I was arrested. We were military medics and put in a request for discharge. They didn't tell us we didn't have a choice. They rounded up six of my colleagues and we were put on a plane to Xieng Khouang. When we arrived, we realized it was prison. We were in shock. As they read our crimes to us, they accused us of political treason. "You wanted to be too free," they concluded. We didn't know what we did wrong. They chained our hands and legs and imprisoned us for four years. In prison, we had to do everything from growing produce, building homes to delivering babies. Whatever they wanted us to, we had to do it.

One summer, Dr. Vannarath, who was a surgeon and head of Mahasot Hospital in Vientiane, came to visit Xieng Khouang hospital in Phonsavan. Back in Vientiane, I was good friends with him. We played tennis and ping pong almost every day after my studies. By the time he came, only six of us medics were left. Three of us were able to escape and see him at the hospital. He was surprised but asked us to be patient. "I'll fight for you," he assured us.

My feeling of discouragement never went away after I was imprisoned. When I got to the refugee camp in Nakhon Phanom, I met my wife and we got married. In the camps, to hold a fresh set of clothes felt good to me. It filled me with happiness. Even if I had to die there in Thailand, I told myself I wouldn't care — anything to leave Laos.

We resettled in Minnesota in 1983. I was excited to buy my first car. It was a small 1980 Dodge. I had been going to ESL class and after three months of schooling, a man from the government center told me I'd be going to vocational school, which was a program for refugees who wanted to become nurses. It was sponsored by the University of Minnesota.

I told them my English isn't good. He said it was good enough.

———

*ຊັບ ສ, ອາຍຸ **64** ປີ
Minneapolis

ຊັບ ເຕີບໃຫຍ່ຢູ່ແຂວງອັດຕະປື, ຊ່ວງປີດປ່ອຍຈາກສະທະພາບຝຣັ່ງເສດ ໃນປີ 1954. ຊັບ ເປັນຜູ້ ຊ່ວຍແພດຢູ່ ສປປ ລາວ ກ່ອນທີ່ຈະຍົກຍ້າຍໄປຢູ່ເມືອງມິນີເຮັປໂປລິດ ແລະ ໄດ້ເປັນພະຍາບານຕັ້ງແຕ່ ນັ້ນມາ. ຊັບ ພັກອາໄສກັບພັນລະຍາຂອງລາວຢູ່ເມືອງມິນເນໂປລິດ.

ຂ້າພະເຈົ້າເຕີບໃຫຍ່ຢູ່ແຂວງອັດຕະປື ຈົນຮອດອາຍຸ 12 ປີໄດ້ຖືກຍົກຍ້າຍໄປຢູ່ເມືອງປາກເຊ ແລະ ຮຽນ ຈົບມັດທະຍົມຢູ່ນັ້ນ ແລະ ໃນ ຂະນະຽດ ຮັບກັບສິ່ງຄວາມກໍ່າລັງເລີ່ມຮຸນແຮງ. ຄວາມຊົງຈຳ ຂອງຂ້າພະເຈົ້າ ແມ່ນ ກ່ຽວການເຕີບໃຫຍ່ ຄາມກາງສາງ ບຶນ, ສຽງລະເບີດ ແລະ ສະມາຊິກໃນຄອບຄົວ ລົ້ມຕາຍ ຍ້ອນສົ່ງຄາມ ນັ້ນ. ໃນລະຫວ່າງໆ 1963 – 1964, ແລະ ຂ້າພະເຈົ້າກໍ່າລັງຮຽນຫ້ອງ ປ. 5, ສິ່ງຄວາມກໍ່ໄດ້ທະວີຄວາມ ຮຸນແຮງຂຶ້ນ.

ຕອນຂ້າພະເຈົ້າຍັງນ້ອຍຢູ່ ຂ້ອຍມີຫຍັງໃຫ້ເຮັດຫຼາຍປານໃດ, ໝູ່ບ້ານພວກເຮົາທຸກຍາກທຸກທຸກ, ບໍ່ມີນ້ຳສະ ອາດໄວ້ໃຊ້, ບໍ່ມີທໍ່ຂອງນ້ຳ, ບໍ່ມີການເທພື້ນໃດໆ ເປັນພຽງແຕ່ດີນແດງເທົ່ານັ້ນ ແລະ ມັນເປັນບ່ອນມີພໍ່ແມ່ ຂອງຂ້າພະເຈົ້າຊຸກຫຼົບເພື່ອໄວ້ລີ້ໄພ.

ປີ 1968, ປະເທດລາວກໍໄດ້ເຂົ້າມາຍຶດເອົາແຂວງຂອງພວກເ ຮົາ, ເຮົາເຈົ້າສົ່ງເດັກນ້ອຍພາຍໃນໝູ່ບ້ານໃຫ້ ໄປຢູ່ສູນທີ່ເມືອງປາກເຊ ເພື່ອໃຫ້ທ່າງໄກ້ຈາກເຂດສົ່ງຄວາມ. ພວກເຮົາຕ້ອງໄດ້ທ່າງໄກຈາກພໍ່ແມ່ ແລະ ຂ້າ ພະເຈົ້າເອງໄດ້ຢູ່ສະຖານທີ່ນັ້ນເປັນເວລາ 3 ປີ. ຊ່ວງຫຼຸມນ້ອຍ, ພວກເຮົາບໍ່ຢາກສຳນຶກວ່າເກີດ ຫຍັງຂຶ້ນແພ່, ຫຼື ວ່າຄອບຄົວຂອງພວກເຮົາຢູ່ຄັບທຸກຊີວິດບໍ່. ສອບຂ້າພະເຈົ້າເອງກໍສົນໃຈ ແຕ່ຮຽນຂັ້ງສີ ແລະ ຫຼົ້ນກິຕາ, ແຕະບາດໃນເວລາທ່າງໆ.

ຂ້າພະເຈົ້າເຂົ້າບັນຈຸໂຮງຮຽນແພດສາດໃນລະຫວ່າງໆປີ 1972 – 1976 ເພື່ອຮຽນເປັນຜູ້ຊ່ວຍແພດ ແລະ ໃນເວລາຕໍ່ມາໃນປີ 1976 ຂ້າພະເຈົ້າກໍຈົບການສຶກສາ ແລະ ກໍຖືກຈັບກຸມໃນເວລາໆອກັບ ຍ້ອນ ເຫດຜົນທີ່ວ່າ ພວກເຮົາບໍ່ຢາກລອອກຈາກການເປັນແພດທະຫານ. ພວກເຮົາບໍ່ໄດ້ບອກໄວ້ພວກເຮົາເລີຍວ່າພວກເຮົາບໍ່ສາມາດເລືອກໄດ້. ພຽງແຕ່ຈັບຕົວພວກເຮົາ 6 ຄົນ ຂຶ້ນຍົບໄປແຂວງຫຼວງຕ່າງໆ, ແລະ ຕອນຮອດພວ ກເຮົາຈິ່ງຮູ້ວ່າເຮົາເຈົ້າຈັບພວກເຮົາມາຄຸມຂັງ. ເຮົາເຈົ້າກ່າວຫາວ່າພວກເຮົາເປັນ

———

ກະບົດທາງການເມືອງ ແລະ ພວກເຮົາ "ຢາກເປັນອິດສະລະໂພດ." ຕອນຢູ່ໃນຄຸກ ນັ້ນພວກເຮົາຕ້ອງເຮັດໝົດທຸກຢ່າງທີ່ເຂົາເຈົ້າສັ່ງໃຫ້ເຮັດ, ຕັ້ງແຕ່ປູກຝັ່ງ, ປູກເຮືອນ, ແລະ ປະສູດເດັກນ້ອຍ.

ມັ້ນພຽງໃນຊ່ວງພັກແລ້ວ, ຂ້າໄດ້ພົບໝູ່ຜູ້ໜຶ່ງຊື່ ຕຣ. ອັນບະລາດ ທໍ່ຫຍ້າຜ້າຕັດຢູ່ໂຮງໝັມະໂຫສົດ ທີ່ນະ ຄອບທຸວງວຽງຈັນ ເຜິ່ນໄດ້ຂຶ້ນມາຢູ່ມຍ ງາໂຮງໝໍ່ຢູ່ເມືອງໂພນສະທວັນ, ແຂວງຽງວຽງໆ. ພວກເຮົາ ເຄີຍຕຶ່ງເທນມິດ ແລະ ບໍ່ງປ່ອງບຳກັບສະໄໝກ່ອນຢູ່ວຽງຈັນ. ຕອນທີ່ ຕຣ ເຜິ່ນມາຍາມ, ພວກເຮົາເຫຼືອກັບແຕ່ 6 ຄົນ, ແລະ ສາມຄົນພວກເຮົາໄດ້ພາກັບພີໍອອກໄປຫາເຜິ່ ນຢູ່ໂຮງໝໍ. ເຜິ່ນຕິໃຈທຫາຍທີ່ເຫັນພວກເຮົາ ແຕ່ ເຜິ່ນກໍ່ໃຫ້ຄຳໝັ້ນສັນຍາວ່າຈະ ຊ່ວຍພວກເຮົາອອກໄປໃຫ້ໄດ້.

ຄວາມຮູ້ສຶກທໍ່ແທ້ກໍ່ເຄີຍອອກໄປຈາກໃຈຂ້າພະເຈົ້າເລີຍຕອບທີ່ຍັງຖືກຂັງຢູ່ຄຸກ ແລະ ໃນທີ່ສຸດຂ້າພະເຈົ້າ ກໍ່ສາມາດໜີໄປສູບອົບພະຍົກ ທີ່ນະຄອບພະນົມ ແລະ ຂ້າພະເຈົ້າກໍ່ໄດ້ພົບພັບລະຍາຢູ່ທັ້ນ ແລ້ວກໍ່ໄດ້ ແຕ່ງງານກັບລາວ. ຢູ່ ໃນສູບພວກເຮົາໄດ້ເຄື່ອງບຸ່ງໃໝ່, ມັນເຮັດໃຫ້ຂ້າພະເຈົ້າມີຄວາມສຸກຫຼາຍ; ຂ້າພະເຈົ້າຍັງເຄີຍຄິດວ່າ ຖ້າຊີວິດຂ້າພະເຈົ້າຕ້ອງຈົບຢູ່ປະເທດໄທ ກໍ່ຄົງຍັງດີກ່າວຕ້ອງຢູ່ປະເທດລາວ.

ຊຸມປີ 1983, ພວກເຮົາກໍ່ໄດ້ອົບພະຍົກມາລັດມິນີໂຊຕ້າ. ຂ້າພະເຈົ້າຮູ້ລີ ດຄັບທຳຮິດເປັນລົດ ດອດຈ ລຸ້ນປີ 1980. ຂ້າພະເຈົ້າຕ້ອງໄດ້ເຂົ້າຮຽນ ກຸມພາສາອັງກິດເປັນເວລາ 3 ເດືອນ ແລະ ມັ້ນພຽງເຈົ້າຫ້າທີ່ຂອງສູບ ລັດຖະບານກໍ່ມາບອກຂ້າພະເຈົ້າວ່າ ຂ້າພະເຈົ້າສາມາດໄປຮຽນຕໍ່ຢູ່ໂຮງຮຽນວິຊາ ຊີບ ທີ່ເປັນອົບພະຍົກສາມາດໄປຮຽນເພື່ອມາເປັນພະຍາບານ, ເຊິ່ງເປັນການຮຸກຢູ່ ຂອງມະຫາວິທະຍາໄລມິນີໂຊຕ້າ.

ຂ້າພະເຈົ້າເວົ້າໄທບລາວ່າ, ພາສາອັງກິດຂອງຂ້າພະເຈົ້າບໍ່ເກັ່ງ ແລະ ລາວກໍ່ຕອບວ່າ ມັນພຽງພໍແລ້ວ.

Name and identifiers have been changed under storyteller's request.

CEASEFIRE (Suggested for use with Viet-Asia by James P. Sterba)
NYT-05-12/8/72-Vientaine: From left, King Savang Vatthana of Laos,
his son, the Crown Prince Vong Savang, and U.S. Ambassador G. MacMurtie
Godley watching American aerial performance during a fair. At right is
Prince Souvanna Phouma, Prime Minister of Laos, at same fair.

My mother fell in love with a cake decorator amidst post-war Viet Nam

post 1975

Image courtesy of Sang Trương

LIVE WITH COURAGE AND COMPASSION

Sống can đảm và nhân hậu

Sang Trương, 84
Saint Paul

Binh Duong is a town about thirty kilometers from Saigon, Việt Nam. I was born there in the year of 1935. Later, my family and I moved to Saigon due to the job demand and further education in a foreign language.

My new dwelling was in Hoa Hung, District 10, about three kilometers from Saigon market. There was a rich French quarter in this location with villas painted in red color surrounded by banana trees. I originated from a wealthy and French influenced background.

During the Việt Nam War, I worked as a stenographer, translator and interpreter for the United States (US). I had good fluency in English, French and Việt. I immigrated to the US as a high-ranking employee under the sponsorship of the US Department of Defense.

During the time I was with the US military in Việt Nam, I worked with various Việt Ministries. I would obtain various important documents from Việt offices for the US Officers to work on.

In my life, I luckily escaped death many times. When I was 9 years old, I loved to swim. Despite the warning from my parents, one day I swam in my hometown river with one of my young friends. My friend pushed me down deep under the water, causing me to almost drown. Luckily, I was able to save myself by moving up from the water.

Another drama happened to me. During the time I was with the US military office, my American boss and I went to the US Embassy in Saigon to attend a meeting. When they arrived there, suddenly, I had a headache. Feeling tired, I asked my boss to be able to get off earlier. When they moved out of the Embassy, she saw many ambulance cars blowing their horns and rushed into the Embassy. There was an explosion there because Communist terrorists used bombs to attack it. Many people died in that chaos. That was the second time I escaped death.

In 1975, after the communist forces occupied Saigon, I tried to go to the airport to board the plane to go to the United States, but it was bombed. So, I had to run home and stayed hidden in Buddhist temples where I studied English and practiced Buddhism. I never lost hope, but still had a beautiful picture in my mind that one day I might reach America. Hope helped me survive during the difficult days living under communist regime.

A very good chance came to me later. One day, when I was biking on the street, I saw an American sitting on a cyclo driven by a Việt person. He was trying to find the way to Caravel Hotel but the cyclo driver could not speak English. I helped him out by showing the way. My manners and fluency in English had been developed from my involvement with the US military, and he knew right away. He invited me to the hotel for a meal.

Arriving at the hotel, I gave photocopies of the Certificates of Commendation I obtained to the American. I then found out that he was a major in the US Army. He felt very sorry for me that I still had to live in a Việt Nam that was very dangerous for me.

Arriving back home in the US, he contacted my old boss and found out that he had become a major general working in Washington, D.C. When contacted, the general told him he was very glad that I was still alive. He thought I had died in the chaos of the war. He told me he would help me out of Việt Nam.

One month later, I arrived in the US. I went to Seattle first, and later came to live in Minnesota to reunite with my children living there.

My advice for healing is to lead a courageous life, have hope, and patience. Always strive forward with no fear. Besides that, I have a heart full of compassion. I have been diligently helping many people in need here due to lack of understanding of the English language.

My legacy is to live with courage and compassion. Open our heart wide to help others. Try to bring honor to Việt Nam. The Việt people are courageous, protect each other and bring honor to our country.

—

Sang Trương, 84
Saint Paul

Tôi sanh vào năm 1935, tại tỉnh Bình Dương khoảng ba mươi cây số cách Sài Gòn, Việt-Nam. Sau đó, tôi và gia đình dọn về Sài-Gòn do nhu cầu công việc và học thêm ngoại ngữ.

Chỗ trú ngụ mới của tôi ở Hòa Hưng, Quận 10, khoảng ba cây số cách chợ Sài-Gòn. Nơi đây, có một khu vực giàu có của người dân Pháp trú ngụ, gồm có nhiều biệt thự bao quanh bởi những cây chuối. Tôi xuất thân từ một gia đình giàu ảnh hưởng Pháp quốc.

Trong chiến tranh Việt-Nam, tôi làm Bí Thư Tốc ký viên, và Thông Dịch Viên/Thông Ngôn cho vị Giám Đốc Phòng Tham Mưu Quân Pháp, Bộ Tư Lệnh Phái Đoàn Cố Vấn Quân Sự Hoa Kỳ tại Việt-Nam. Tôi rất thông thạo về Anh Ngữ, Pháp Ngữ và Việt Ngữ. Tôi nhập cư vào Hoa Kỳ với sự bảo trợ của Bộ Quốc Phòng Hoa Kỳ.

Trong chiến tranh Việt-Nam, tôi làm việc giúp cho Quân Đội Hoa Kỳ với nhiều văn phòng Việt-Nam. Tôi thu được nhiều tài liệu quan trọng từ các văn phòng đó để cho các Sĩ Quan Hoa Kỳ có thể làm việc.

Trong đời sống, tôi may mắn thoát chết nhiều lần. Khi lên 9 tuổi, tôi rất thích bơi lội. Mặc dầu cha mẹ cảnh cáo, vào một ngày tôi lội tấm dưới sông ở quê nhà với một người bạn. Tôi bị bạn nhận chìm xuống nước gần bị chết đuối. May mắn thay, tôi ngoi lên được trên mặt nước và thoát nạn.

Một thảm cảnh khác lại đến với Tôi. Trong thời gian làm việc với Văn Phòng Quân Đội Hoa Kỳ, vào một ngày nọ, tôi và Ông Giám Đốc đến Toà Đại Sứ Hoa Kỳ để dự một phiên họp. Khi đến nơi, bất thình lình tôi bị nhức đầu. Cảm thấy mệt, tôi nói với Ông Giám Đốc đi ra ngoài. Khi ra khỏi Toà Đại Sứ, tôi thấy nhiều xe cứu thương huýt còi và chạy vào Sứ Quán đã bị

nổ tung do khủng bố cộng sản đặt bom. Có rất nhiều người chết trong cuộc hỗn loạn đó. Đó là lần thứ hai tôi thoát chết.

Vào năm 1975, khi Cộng Sản xâm chiếm Sài-Gòn, tôi cố gắng đi ra phi trường để đáp phi cơ sang Hoa Kỳ, nhưng phi trường bị pháo kích nặng nề. Tôi đành phải chạy về nhà và vào chùa Phật Giáo ẩn nấp. Nơi đây tôi ôn học Anh Ngữ và tu tập Phật pháp. Tôi không bao giờ chịu thất vọng, vẫn giữ trong tâm một hình ảnh đẹp là một ngày nào đó tôi có thể đến Hoa Kỳ. Niềm hy vọng giúp tôi sinh tồn trong những ngày gặp khó khăn phải sống dưới chế độ cộng sản.

Sau đó, một dịp may đến với tôi. Một ngày nọ, khi đang đạp xe ngoài đường phố, tôi gặp một người Hoa Kỳ ngồi trên chiếc xích lô do một người Việt Nam đạp xe. Ông muốn đến Khách Sạn Ca-ra-queo nhưng người đạp xe không hiểu Anh Ngữ. Tôi đến giúp chỉ đường cho người Hoa Kỳ. Vì nói được tiếng Anh trôi chảy và mang phong cách của một nhân viên làm việc lâu ngày với quân Đội Hoa Kỳ, người Mỹ này nhận ra được tôi có làm việc với quân đội Hoa Kỳ. Ông mời tôi đến khách sạn để đãi ăn.

Đến khách sạn, tôi mang những phóng ảnh của các Bằng Khen Thưởng ông Giám Đốc cấp tại văn phòng Hoa Kỳ cho Ông này. Tôi cũng nhận ra được Ông là Thiếu Tá làm việc với Quân Đội Hoa Kỳ tại Việt-Nam. Ông rất lấy làm ái ngại cho tôi vẫn còn ở nước của cộng sản rất nguy hiểm cho tôi.

Khi trở về Hoa Kỳ, Ông liên lạc được với ông Giám Đốc của tôi và biết rằng Ông hiện là Trung Tướng làm việc tại Văn Phòng Bộ Tư Lệnh Tham Mưu Quân Pháp tại Hoa Kỳ. Trung Tướng cho Ông biết Ông rất mừng tôi vẫn còn sống. Ông nghĩ rằng tôi đã qua đời trong cơn hỗn loạn của chiến tranh và bảo sẽ giúp tôi thoát khỏi nước cộng sản.

Một tháng sau, tôi qua được Hoa Kỳ. Tôi đến Seattle trước nhất, và sau đó đến sống tại Minnesota để đoàn tụ với các con đang sống tại đây.

Lời khuyên của tôi là để chữa lành ta phải sống can đảm, có niềm tin, và lòng kiên nhẫn. Luôn tiến đến phía trước không sợ sệt. Ngoài ra, tôi còn có một con tim đầy yêu thương. Tôi đã tích cực giúp rất nhiều người cần được giúp đỡ do kém hiểu biết về Anh Ngữ.

Lời Di Huấn của tôi là: Hãy sống với lòng can đảm và tình yêu thương. Mở rộng con tim để giúp đỡ những người khác, cố gắng mang vinh hạnh về cho đất nước. Theo tôi, người Việt Nam đầy lòng can đảm, luôn hoàn thiện bản thân, và mang vinh hạnh về cho đất nước.

United States Senate
WASHINGTON, DC 20510-2303

November 15, 1994

Dear Ms. Truong:

Recently I learned about your many achievements at the University of Minnesota. My warmest congratulations to you.

I was moved by the fact that you arrived in Minnesota only twenty months ago and have already made a new life with your family. I commend your desire to receive a strong education and your activism in the community. In addition, I was excited to learn that you received a General College Scholarship for 1994-95.

I wish you the very best as you pursue your dream to serve the country with pride. I have no doubt that you will achieve this goal. It is people like you that help to make Minnesota the great state that it is.

My very best to you and your family.

Sincerely,

Paul David Wellstone
United States Senator

1980s - 2000s

Survival of Southeast Asian American youth in the form of local gangs in Los Angeles and all over the U.S.

Image courtesy of Phillipe Thao

CONCEPT OF HMONG AND HOME

Hmoob thiab Hmoob lub Tsev

Phillipe Thao, 22
Chicago, IL

76

For a people with no homeland, the concept of home has always been an integral part of Hmong culture. During the Vietnam War, the diaspora caused many to reinvent their homes in new and foreign lands. When one's spirit drifts away, a shaman calls it back home into the body. As a second-generation gay Hmong man who grew up in the white suburbs of the Twin Cities, I was eager to leave my home in order to be around those that accepted my sexuality.

Whether it was getting mocked as a child for sewing paj ntaub or choreographing traditional dances to Maiv Muas music videos, I felt like my sexuality was not welcomed in my culture. At eighteen, I moved to Chicago for college. I explored my sexuality, fell in love for the first time, and surrounded myself with a queer chosen family. For the first time, I was myself.

During Thanksgiving break of 2015, my mother asked if I would like to come out to all of my closest relatives. In Hmong culture, family is everything. My parents wanted to come out to everyone as a family, rather than have people gossip about my sexuality through the grapevine. I had built up so much anger and resentment toward my culture for its intolerance of queerness, but I ultimately agreed.

Over twenty of my closest relatives gathered around a long table filled with food, none of them aware as to why my parents had invited them to this gathering. My father thanked everyone for coming, and then he looked at me and I knew it was my cue. In Hmong language, there is no word for "gay," but slowly and surely I confidently came out to everyone at that table. And one by one, every single relative went around the table and voiced their love and support for me. A few of them even cried tears of happiness for me, and I had never experienced unconditional love that deep. That was a pivotal moment in my life because not only did my family come out together, but being embraced by my relatives' love, some of whom were immigrants and uneducated about sexuality, brought me back home — to my family, and to my Hmong culture.

Diaspora bleeds into subsequent generations, but it is through this diaspora that we realize the intersectionality of our identities.

———

Phillipe Thoj, 22
Chicago, IL

Rau ib co neeg uas tsis muaj teb chaws, lub vaj lub tse yeej ib txwm yog ib qho ua tseem ceeb rau peb Hmoob kab lig kev cai. Lub sij hawm thaum Nyab Laj ua tsov rog, coob leej tau tawg mus nyob rau ub rau no sib nrhoj sib nrhas. Nyias thiaj li tau mus ua vaj ua tsev dua tshlab rau lwm daim av lawm. Thaum ib tug ntsuj plig tsis puab cev lawm, tus niam neeb los sis txiv neeb yuav tsum tau hu tus ntsuj tus ntsuj plig kom rov qab los vaj los tsev, los puab tus neeg ntawv lub cev. Vim kuv yog ib tug tub Hmoob uas nyiam txiv neej, thiab kuv tau tuaj loj hlob nrog Meskas dawb nyob ntawm lub Nroog Ntxaib, kuv xav tawm ntawm kuv lub tsev mus nrhiav cov neeg uas to taub thiab txhawb nqa kuv txoj kev nyiam txiv neej.

Thaum kuv tseem me, luag yeej saib tsis taus kuv vim kuv tau ua paj ntaub losis huab las voos rau Maiv Muas cov nkauj. Kuv yeej xav tau hais tias Hmoob kab lig kev cai tsis txais tos ib tug neeg coj li kuv. Thaum kuv muaj 18 xyoo, kuv tau mus nyob rau lub nroog Chicago mus kawm ntawv qib siab. Kuv tau muaj lub sij hawm los soj ntsuam xyuas kuv tus kheej qhov uas kuv nyiam txiv neej. Kuv tau paub txog kev sib hlub thawj thawj zaug nyob rau hauv kuv lub neej. Kuv kuj tau los nyob nrog ib tse neeg uas txawv txawv li kuv. Qhov no yog thawj

thawj zaug nyob rau hauv kuv lub neej uas kuv thiaj li tau yog kuv tus kheej.

Luj sij hawm Thanksgiving break nyob rau xyoo 2015, kuv niam tau nug kuv hais tias seb kuv puas xav los tsev, los tawm suab qhia txog kuv txoj kev nyiam txiv neej rau kuv tej txheeb tej ze. Raws li peb Hmoob txoj kev ntseeg, yus tsev neeg yog txhua tsav txhua yam. Kuv niam thiab kuv txiv nkawv xav kom kuv los fim txhua leej txhua tus li ib tse neeg. Tej lus paj lus cua txog ntawm kuv txoj kev uas nyiam txiv neej, nkawv tsis xav kom muaj ntxiv lawm. Vim kuv txoj kab lig kev cai tsis txais tos cov tib neeg txawv txawv li kuv, kuv tau muaj kev chim thiab kev ntxub rau kuv txoj kab lig kev cai ntau heev los lawm, tiam sis txog thaum kawg kuv kuj pom zoo nrog kuv niam lawm thiab.

Ntau tshaj nees nkaum leej ntawm kuv tej txheeb tej ze tau tuaj zaum ncig peb ib lub rooj uas muaj zaub muaj mov. Lawv tsis muaj leej twg yuav paub hais tias yog vim li cas kuv niam thiab kuv txiv nkawv ho caw kom sawv daws tuaj. Kuv txiv tau ua tsaug rau txhuas txhuas tus uas tuaj, tas ces nws tau ntsia kuv. Lub sib hawm ntawv ces kuv twb paub hais tias txog kuv zeeg lawm. Nyob rau hauv lus Hmoob peb yeej tsis muaj ib los lus rau "gay", tiam sis vim kuv maj mam qhia thiab vim kuv ntseeg kuv tus kheej, kuv kuj qhia tau tawm rau lawv lawm hais tias kuv yog ib tug tub Hmoob uas nyiam txiv neej. Ib tug dhau ib tug, nyias tau hais nyias txoj kev hlub thiab kev txhawb nqa rau kuv. Muaj ob peb tug tseem ua kua muag poob dawb vog vim lawv zoo siab nrog kuv. Kuv yeej tsis tau txais ib txoj kev hlub tob thiab zoo npaum li no nyob hauv kuv lub neej li. Lub sib hawm ntawv yog ib lub sij hawm uas zoo tshaj plaws nyob rau hauv kuv lub neej, vim hais tias twb tsis yog kuv tsev neeg xwb uas tau tawm qhib suav txhawb nqa kuv, tiam sis kuv tej txheeb tej ze los qhib siab lug muab lawv txoj kev hlub rau kuv. Txawm hais tias ib co ntawm kuv tej txheeb tej ze yuav yog neeg poob teb chaws thiab tsis paub txog tej kev uas txawv txawv li txiv neej nyiam txiv neej, los lawv sawv daws txoj kev hlub tau cawm kuv, tau coj kuv rov los txog kuv lub vaj lub tsev, txog kuv tsev neeg, thiab txog kuv txoj kab lig kev cai Hmoob.

Niaj hnub niam no, peb cov me nyuam Hmoob lawv tsis nyob rau tej qub chaw nyob uas lawv niam lawv txiv ib txwm nyob lawm, tiam sis lawv txoj kev tawm mus nyob rau lwm qhov chaw yog ib txoj kev uas yuav ua rau lawv ras thiab paub txog tias lawv yog leej twg.

1990

— My parents
came to the U.S.

:)

DOUBLE DISPLACEMENT

ការផ្លាស់កន្លែងទ្វេដង

Ched Nin, 39
Farmington

My name is Ched Nin. I am a father, I am an activist and I am a refugee. My family fled their native country of Cambodia to live in a refugee camp in Thailand where I was born. Then we were transferred to the Philippines. At the age of 6 years old, my family and I came to the United States in 1986.

In 1979, my mother gave birth to me in Prachinburi, Thailand and I spent the first few years of my life in Khao-I-Dang refugee camp, then on a military base in the Philippines. My earliest memories of my childhood are waiting for the food drop in the Philippines to get first dibs on the banana coconut ice cream block.

During my first year in the United States of America, we lived in Seattle, Washington for few months, then moved to Rochester until I was 9 years old and then to Faribault, Minnesota. My father worked as a janitor at IBM and then the Faribault canning company and my mother work at Jenny-O Turkey Corporation. In my humble beginning, we all lived together under one roof, which is true to this day. I am now the head of my household and provide for my parents, wife, and children. We all are living in a small community south of the river in Farmington, Minnesota. I am working hard to provide for my family as a first generation immigrant. Currently, I work as a carpenter at Northside Construction under the Local 322 Carpenters Union.

In search of love and happiness, I found an opportunity for me and my children. My kids are well educated, I found employment, unexpectedly I also found love. I married my wife Jenny Srey on September 5, 2015. She is the love of my

life. She is beautiful and well-liked by others. She tells me she found me attractive because I'm good with kids and have a great sense of humor. We have been married for three years and we are currently raising our children in the rural town of Farmington. Recently, we welcomed our youngest son, Khameron, to our family.

In recent years I was faced with the fear of deportation. It was a double displacement because I consider America my home. Cambodia, Thailand, and the Philippines are my stepping stone countries that birthed my early childhood. My future and present are rooted in America and I consider myself an Asian American or "Khmerican". This is my home now.

My journey to America is a fine one. I am honored and grateful for the support from our Khmer community.

In return, my goal and passion are to help the Khmer community by educating about a pathway to citizenship and voting rights. I also want to work as an activist for deportees and engage the public to participate in local and national elections. I want to encourage our Khmer community to voice their concerns and be a voice to change policy such as criminal justice reform.

———

ចិត នីន, 39
Farmington

ខ្ញុំឈ្មោះ ចិត នីន។ ខ្ញុំគឺជាឪពុកម្នាក់ ខ្ញុំគឺជាសកម្មជនម្នាក់ ហើយខ្ញុំគឺជាជនភៀសខ្លួនម្នាក់។ គ្រួសាររបស់ខ្ញុំ បានភៀសខ្លួនពីប្រទេស កម្ពុជា ជាមាតុភូមិកំណើតរបស់គេ ដើម្បីទៅរស់នៅក្នុងជំរំជនភៀស ខ្លួន ក្នុងប្រទេសថៃ ជាកន្លែងដែលខ្ញុំបានកើត។ ជាបន្ទាប់មកទៀត យើងក៏បានប្ដូរកន្លែង ទៅប្រទេសភីលីពីន។ នៅពេលអាយុប្រាំមួយឆ្នាំ គ្រួសាររបស់ខ្ញុំ និងខ្ញុំ បានមកដល់សហរដ្ឋ ក្នុងឆ្នាំ 1986។

នៅឆ្នាំ 1979 ម្ដាយរបស់ខ្ញុំបានឲ្យកំណើតខ្ញុំ នៅក្នុងជំរំប្រាជិនប៊ុរី ប្រទេសថៃ ហើយខ្ញុំបានចំណាយពេលប៉ុន្មានឆ្នាំដំបូង នៃជីវិតរបស់ខ្ញុំ នៅក្នុងជំរំជនភៀសខ្លួន ខៅអ៊ីដាង និងបន្ទាប់មកទៀត នៅឯបន្ទាយទាហានមួយ ក្នុងប្រទេសភីលីពីន។ អនុស្សាវរីយ៍នៃកុមារភាព ដំបូងរបស់ខ្ញុំ គឺរង់ចាំការទំលាក់ម្ហូបអាហារ នៅប្រទេសភីលីពីន ដើម្បីឲ្យបានស្គាល់រសជាតិ ដុំការ៉េមក៏ខ្ទិះចេក និងដូង។

នៅក្នុងអំឡុងឆ្នាំដំបូងរបស់ខ្ញុំ នៅក្នុងសហរដ្ឋអាមេរិក យើងបានរស់នៅក្រុង Seattle រដ្ឋ Washington ចំនួនប៉ុន្មានខែ និងបន្ទាប់មកទៀត ក៏បានផ្លាស់ទៅក្រុង Rochester រហូតដល់ខ្ញុំមានអាយុ ៩ ឆ្នាំ និងបន្ទាប់មកទៀត បានផ្លាស់ទៅក្រុង Faribault រដ្ឋ Minnesota។ ឪពុករបស់ខ្ញុំ បានធ្វើការជាអ្នកបាចសំអាច នៅក្រុមហ៊ុន IBM និងបន្ទាប់មកទៀត ទៅក្រុមហ៊ុនផលិតកំប៉ុងនៅក្រុង Faribault វិញម្ដង។ របស់ខ្ញុំវិញ បានធ្វើការនៅសាជីវកម្ម Jenny-O Turkey។ ក្នុងការរស់នៅខូរបស់ខ្ញុំ នៅដើមដំបូងយើងបានរស់នៅជុំគ្នាទាំងអស់ ក្នុងជួ ទៃតមួយមកដល់សព្វថ្ងៃនេះ។ នៅឥឡូវនេះ ខ្ញុំគឺជាមេគ្រួសាររបស់ខ្ញុំ និងផ្ដត់ផ្គង់សំរាប់ឪពុកម្ដាយរបស់ខ្ញុំ ប្រពន្ធនិងកូនៗរបស់ខ្ញុំ យើងទាំងអស់គ្នា កំពុងតែរស់នៅក្នុងសហគមន៍មួយជាមួយគ្នា ស្ថិតនៅភាគខាងត្បូងនៃស្ទឹងក្នុងក្រុង Farmington រដ្ឋ Minnesota។ ខ្ញុំខំប្រឹងធ្វើការ ដើម្បីផ្ដត់ផ្គង់សំរាប់គ្រួសារ ជាជនអន្តោប្រវេសន៍ជំនាន់ដំបូង។ នៅពេលបច្ចុប្បន្ននេះ ខ្ញុំធ្វើការជាជាងឈើ នៅក្រុមហ៊ុន Northside Construction នៅក្រោមសហជីព Carpenters តំបន់ 322។

ក្នុងការស្វែងរកសេចក្ដីស្រឡាញ់ និងសុភមង្គល ខ្ញុំក៏បានរកឃើញឧបសគ្គសមួយ សំរាប់ខ្ញុំ និងកូនៗរបស់ខ្ញុំ។ កូនៗរបស់ខ្ញុំបានទទួលការអប់រំ យ៉ាងល្អ ខ្ញុំក៏បានការងារធ្វើ និងដោយមិនបានរើស ខ្ញុំក៏បានរកឃើញសេចក្ដីស្រឡាញ់ដែរ។ ខ្ញុំបានរៀបអាពាហ៍ពិពាហ៍ ជាមួយនឹងប្រពន្ធ របស់ខ្ញុំ ឈ្មោះចន្ថនី ស្រី កាលពីថ្ងៃទី ៥ ខែកញ្ញា 2015។ នាងគឺជាមនុស្សជាទីស្រឡាញ់ នៃជីវិតរបស់ខ្ញុំ នាងគឺស្មោះត្រង់ ហើយ មនុស្សងទៀត។ ក៏ចូលចិត្តនាងដែរ។ នាងប្រាប់ខ្ញុំ ថានាងបានរកឃើញខ្ញុំ ជាទីជាប់ចិត្ត ពីព្រោះខ្ញុំជាមនុស្សល្អជាមួយនឹងក្មេងៗ និងពូកែ ធ្វើឱ្យមនុស្សសប្បាយចិត្ត។ យើងទាំងពីរនាក់ បានរៀបអាពាហ៍ពិពាហ៍និងគ្នាចំនួនបីឆ្នាំ ហើយនៅបច្ចុប្បន្ននេះ យើងកំពុងតែចិញ្ចឹមកូន

របស់យើង នៅក្នុងទីក្រុងជនបទ នៃក្រុង Farmington។ នៅពេលថ្មីៗនេះ យើងបានស្វាគមន៍កូនប្រុសពៅរបស់យើង ឈ្មោះខែម៉ារុន មកក្នុងគ្រួសាររបស់យើង។

នៅក្នុងឆ្នាំថ្មីៗនេះ ខ្ញុំបានប្រឈមមុខ ជាមួយនឹងការភ័យខ្លាចពីការនិរទេស។ ខ្ញុំបានជួបប្រទះ នូវការផ្លាស់កន្លែងទៅដង ពីព្រោះតែខ្ញុំចាត់ទុក ប្រទេសអាមេរិក ជាគេហដ្ឋានរបស់ខ្ញុំ។ នៅប្រទេសកម្ពុជា ប្រទេសថៃ និងប្រទេសភីលីពីន គឺជាប្រទេសនៃជំរុំជនជោតគាសា ដែលបាន ឡុកំណើតនៃកុមារភាពដំបូរ របស់ខ្ញុំ។ អនាគតរបស់ខ្ញុំ និងនៅបច្ចុប្បន្ននេះ គឺបានចាក់ឬសនៅក្នុងប្រទេស អាមេរិក ហើយយខ្ញុំចាត់ទុកខ្លួន ខ្ញុំថាជាជនជាតិអាស៊ុ-អាមេរិក ឬ "ខ្មែរអាមេរិក"។ នេះគឺជាគេហរេដ្ឋានរបស់ខ្ញុំ នៅឥឡូវនេះ។

ដំណើររបស់ខ្ញុំមកអាមេរិក គឺជាល្បូប្រណីតមួយ។ ខ្ញុំមានកិត្តិយស និងមានកតញ្ញូតា សំរាប់ការគាំទ្រ ចេញពីសហគមន៍ខ្មែររបស់យើង។

ជាការតបស្នង គោលដៅ និងចំណង់ចិត្តរបស់ខ្ញុំ គឺដើម្បីជួយសហគមន៍ខ្មែរ តាមរយៈការអប់រំ អំពីផ្នែកចំពោះការចូលសញ្ជាតិ និងសិទ្ធិបោះឆ្នោត។ ខ្ញុំក៏ច ង់ធ្វើការជាសកម្មជនម្នាក់ដែរ សំរាប់និរទេសជន និងនាំទ្រ័ភាពជាការណិជន ឡុ ចូលរួមក្នុងការបោះឆ្នោត ក្នុងមូលដ្ឋាន និងជាតិ។ ខ្ញុំចង់ជំរុញទឹកចិត្តសហ គមន៍ខ្មែរ ឡុបពេញញសំឡេងនៃកង្វល់របស់គេ និងជាសំឡេងដើម្បីផ្លាស់ប្ដូរ យោបាយ ដូចជាការវិកែប្រែច្បាប់រុក្រិតម៉៏ខក្រិតផ្ដការម្ម។

MEKONG MEMORIES

From Spring through Summer of 2018, over 100 Hmong, Khmer, Lao and Việt Minnesotans gathered for community conversations in Minneapolis and Saint Paul; hosted and facilitated by SEADS partners. We were present with each other, shared stories and acknowledged each other's truths. We laughed and cried about the past, present and future possibilities together.

Note: historical moments noted on the following timeline are meant to be a snapshot of our shared history, not a comprehensive list.

WHAT
MEMORIES
SHAPED
YOUR LIFE
STORY?

During Colonization

1858–1954
French Indochina colonization of Vietnam, Laos and Cambodia

1941–1945
Japanese briefly occupy Cambodia and Laos

1907
Franco-Siamese Treaty established modern-day Lao borders

1945
Laos independence declared

1947
Hmong were recognized as citizens of Laos

1950
Laos recognized as an independent state by US

1953
Cambodia gained independence from France

1900 ——————————————————————— 1950 ———————

death of my ancestors

OUR PEOPLE COLONIZED AND OCCUPIED BY THE CHINESE, JAPANESE AND FRENCH

birth of my grandparents

I was born.

1954
The Geneva Accords divided Vietnam into two separate countries

1965
Immigration and Nationality Act abolishes national quota system

1964–1973
Operation Barrel Roll: secret bombing of Laos

1970
Cambodian Civil War

1973
Communist Pathet Lao controls government of Laos

Pre-1975

My husband died.

our parents were born

The Mekong waters and fisheries were harmed

WE LIVED NORMAL LIVES BEFORE THE WAR

FAMILIES IMPRISONED

1975

Fall of Phnom Penh

Fall of Saigon

Fall of Vientiane

Southeast Asians flee
Cambodia, Laos and
Vietnam

1976

Socialist Republic of
Vietnam is established

1980

United States Refugee Act of 1980

A growing Khmer-American refugee
population leads to the establishment of
Cambodia Town in Long Beach, CA

1980s–1990s

Social service organizations founded by
Hmong, Khmer, Lao and Viet leaders in
Minnesota

1975 ———————— 1980 ——————————————————————

it was the FALL and BURNING

vientiane, saigon and Phnom Penh was chaos

families separated and lost...

LOVE AND COMFORT FOUND IN Refugee camps

ILLNESS FELL UPON OUR LOVED ONES WITH LACK OF ACCESS TO MEDICINE

1992
Closing of Ban Vinai Refugee camp

United Nations Transitional Authority in Cambodia (UNTAC) is established

1994
Friendship Bridge is opened in Laos between Thailand

Minnesota protests *Miss Saigon* theater production

1996
The Illegal Immigration Reform and Immigrant Responsibility Act of 1996 (IIRIRA) passes, adding penalties that impact thousands of Southeast Asian immigrants living in the US as lawful permanent residents

1997
Laos joins ASEAN

1998
Veterans memorial dedicated to Lao and Hmong veterans in Arlington Cemetery

1999
Minnespta protests *Miss Saigon* theater production

2000
Hmong Veterans Naturalization Act

Luong Ung, Khmer author, publishes *First They Killed My Father*, later adapted into a major Hollywood film

1990 ———— 2000 ————

CARS

AIRPLANES

We arrived to our dreams in America

Resettling across Minnesota plains

HIGHWAYS

2004
Closing of Wat Tham Krabok: 15,000 Hmong resettled in America

Việt American progressive movement significantly grows out of the Bay Area

US normalizes trade relations with Laos

2007
Watt Munisotaram, the largest Cambodian Buddhist temple, is built

2010
United Nations Convention on Cluster Munitions goes into force

First National Lao American Writers Summit in Minneapolis

2011
Death of General Vang Pao

2012
Minnesota crowns its first Lao American as Miss Minnesota

Little Mekong business district in Saint Paul is formed

2013
Minnesota declares May 14 Hmong American Day

Minnesota protests *Miss Saigon* theater production

2015
40th anniversary commemoration events

2016
Barack Obama becomes the first sitting US president to visit Laos

Minnesota memorial dedicated to veterans of the Secret War for Laos

Global Hmong Women's Summit in Thailand

PRESENT

I joined cultur organizations to never forge my traditions and, who I am

CLASH OF CULTURES HAPPENED IN AND OUT OF HOME

I BECAME A MOTHER

I am the first to graduate in my family

I was locked up

2016
Khmer Legacy Museum opens in St. Paul

2017
US Immigration and Customs Enforcement (ICE) detain the well-known "Minnesota 8" Khmer men

2018
16,000+ Southeast Asians received final orders of deportation by US Administration

US Administration imposes visa sanctions on Laos and Myanmar

*June, 24, 2018
SEADS Southeast Asian Convening Conversation

2018

FUTURE

To hold + heal each other.

REWRITING OUR STORIES

Our generation are aware of social justice movements

preserving our mother tongue and culture

IT TAKES A VILLAGE

វិគ្រូវការមួយភូមិ

Vikrak Soth, 38
City of Savage

According to an African proverb, it takes a village to raise a child, and my village included my aunts, my uncle, my grandparents and parents. My name is Virak Soth. I was born in Kao-I-Dang refugee camp, Thailand. At the age of 1, my family and I came to the United States of America in 1981. Later that year we welcomed my American born sister, Sopheap. We initially settled in Minneapolis but moved once I was about to attend school. My parents purchased a home in Edina bordering Minneapolis because they wanted me to have a better education in the suburbs.

Before the war, my parents were raised in a village in Battambang province. My grandfather was a barber and my family were farmers. The times were simple before the Khmer Rouge's civil uprising forever changed their lives as well as our country's future. After the war, my

Image courtesy of Vikrak Soth

family escaped the labor camps, took refuge in Thailand and eventually found our way to America. While we were searching for a permanent home, my family created a village for ourselves.

In America, my father's first job was a candymaker at a chocolate shop and my mother worked as an industrial seamstress in Minneapolis. My childhood memories are fond ones. I remember my first Christmas, an African American man would dress up as Santa Claus and give us toys in our old apartment complex in Minneapolis. One year, I was gifted with a race car as a Christmas present. I was thrilled. The rest of my family were that we were safe in America; sharing food, presents and stories.

I went to school in the Edina school district from kindergarten to twelfth grade. I also furthered my education by attending Saint Olaf College and majoring in Asian studies. College was a great time to discover myself but not everything went as planned. While losing my way academically and having a grandmother needing my assistance, finishing my studies had to wait. I eventually returned and graduated in 2009 after a 7-year hold.

My mother is my source of inspiration. She taught me to be humble, to be brave and to be respectful of others. She was a wonderful cook and many within the community loved and respected her contributions in keeping our Khmer culture alive. We had a close relationship, and I was devastated when she passed away suddenly at the temple in 2012. "Her journey was fulfilled as she died at the holy place where her heart and dedication were held deeply to Buddha," said one of the elders at the hospital. As difficult as it was to accept back then, I understand now that there was no better place that she would have wanted to be when her time came. She will forever be missed.

I want to continue my parents' legacy by creating a village full of love, food and security for my son as well as my extended family. As a 1.5 generation Khmer, I want to help preserve our Buddhist community and teach young Khmer people to not be afraid to ask questions that can lead them to a better understanding of themselves. I also want to help encourage youth to further their education and explore higher learning. Most importantly, I want to share these values that my mother had instilled in me: be humble, be respectful to others and be brave enough to just be.

រ៉ែក ស្រុត្រ, 38
City of Savage

ដោយអាស្រ័យទៅលើសុភាសិតអាប្រាំកំាងមួយ វាគ្រូការមួយភូមិដើម្បីចិញ្ចឹមកូនម្នាក់ ហើយភូមិរបស់ខ្ញុំ រួមមានទាំងមីវរបស់ខ្ញុំ ពូរបស់ខ្ញុំ ជីដូនជីតារបស់ខ្ញុំ និងឪពុកម្តាយរបស់ខ្ញុំ។ ខ្ញុំឈ្មោះវ៉ែក ស្រុត្រ។ ខ្ញុំជានកើតនៅក្នុងជំរំជនភៀសខ្លួន ខេរអីជាង ប្រទេសថៃ។ នៅពេលអាយុ 1 ឆ្នាំ គ្រួសាររបស់ខ្ញុំ និងខ្ញុំ បានមកដល់សហរដ្ឋអាមេរិក ក្នុងឆ្នាំ 1981។ នៅពេលក្រោយមកក្នុងឆ្នាំនោះ យើងក៏បានស្វាគមន៍បូនស្រីរបស់ខ្ញុំ ដែលបានកើតនៅអាមេរិក ឈ្មោះសុភាព។ ជាដំបូង យើងបានតាំងលំនៅក្នុងក្រុង Minneapolis ប៉ុន្តែបានផ្លាស់កន្លែង នៅពេលខ្ញុំបុរងនឹងចូលសាលារៀន។ ឪពុកម្តាយរបស់ខ្ញុំ បានទិញផ្ទះមួយនៅក្នុងក្រុង Edina ជាប្រាំដែននឹងក្រុង Minneapolis ពីព្រោះគាត់បានចង់ឲ្យខ្ញុំមានការអប់រំល្អប្រសើរ នៅក្នុងជាយក្រុង។

នៅពេលមុនសង្គ្រាម ឪពុកម្តាយរបស់ខ្ញុំ បានធំធាត់ឡើងនៅក្នុងភូមិមួយ ក្នុងខេត្របាត់ដំបង។ ជីតារបស់ខ្ញុំ គឺជាជាងកាត់សក់ ហើយ គ្រួសាររបស់ខ្ញុំ គឺជាកសិករ។ ពេលវេលាគឺស្រួល នៅមុនពេលពលរដ្ឋរបស់ខ្មែរក្រហម ធ្វើបបះបោរ ដែលបានដូរជីវិតរបស់គេជាហូត ព្រមទាំងអនាគតនៃ ប្រទេសរបស់យើងដែរ។ បន្ទាប់ពីសង្គ្រាម គ្រួសាររបស់ខ្ញុំបានរត់ គេចពីជំរំលត់ដំ បានជ្រកកោននៅក្នុងប្រទេសថៃ និងមិនឈ្លប់ប៉ុន្មាន ក៏បានរកឃើញផ្លូវរបស់យើង មកកាន់ប្រទេសអាមេរិក។ ក្នុងខណៈ ដែលយើងកំពុងតែស្វែងរកលំនៅជាថិរណ្នេយ៍មួយ គ្រួសាររបស់ខ្ញុំ បានបង្កើតភូមិមួយសំរាប់ខ្លួនយើង។

នៅក្នុងប្រទេសអាមេរិក ការងារដំបូងនៃឪពុករបស់ខ្ញុំ គឺជាអ្នកធ្វើស្ករគ្រាប់ នៅហាងលក់ស៊ុកុឡាមួយ រីឯម្តាយរបស់ខ្ញុំវិញ បានធ្វើការក្នុង ឧស្សាហកម្មជាកាត់ដេរមួយ ក្នុងក្រុង Minneapolis។ អនុស្សារ៉ីយ៍នៃកុមារភាពជំបួងរបស់ខ្ញុំ គឺជាទីចាប់អារម្មណ៍មួយ។ ខ្ញុំនឹកចាំពី បុណ្យណូអែលដំបូងរបស់ខ្ញុំ បុរសអាប្រ៊ិក-អាមេរិកម្នាក់ បានស្ទៀកពាក់សំលៀកបំពាក់ សានតាក្លូស និងបានឲ្យប្រដាប់ក្មេងលេងមកយើង នៅក្នុងផ្ទះល្វែងខ្លស់។ កញ្ចាស់របស់យើង នៅក្នុងក្រុង Minneapolis។ មានឆ្នាំមួយ គេបានទុ យអំណោយខ្ញុំនូវរូបឡានប្រណាំងមួយ ជាអំណោយនៃបុណ្យណូអែល។ ខ្ញុំមានអំណរជាអនេក។ ទាំងអស់គ្នានៃគ្រួសាររបស់ខ្ញុំ បានដឹងថាយើងមានសេចក្តីសុខ នៅប្រទេសអាមេរិក; យើងចែកចាយមួយអាហារ អំណោយ និងរឿង ជាមួយគ្នា។

ខ្ញុំបានទៅសាលា នៅក្នុងមណ្ឌលសាលា Edina ចាប់តាំងពីមតេយ្យសាលា ដល់ថ្នាក់ទីដប់ពីរ។ ខ្ញុំក៏បានទទួលការអប់រំរបស់ខ្ញុំថែមទៀត ដោយទៅរៀននៅមហាវិទ្យាល័យ Saint Olaf និងវិស័យសិក្សាសំខាន់ ក្នុងជនជាតិអាស៊ី។ មហាវិទ្យាល័យ គឺជាពេលមួយដ៏អស្ចារ្យ ដើម្បី

រកឃើញខ្លួនរបស់ខ្ញុំ ប៉ុន្តែអ្វីៗមិនបានកើតឡើងដូចបានគ្រោងទុកឡើយ។ ក្នុងខណៈការបាត់បង់ផ្លូវវិជ្ជាជនរបស់ខ្ញុំ និងមានជំដួនម្នាក់ដែល ត្រូវការជំនួយពីខ្ញុំ ការបញ្ចប់នូវការសិក្សារបស់ខ្ញុំ ត្រូវតែចាំសិន។ មិនយូរប៉ុន្មាន ខ្ញុំក៏បានត្រឡប់ទៅរៀនវិញ និងបានទទួលសញ្ញាប័ត្រក្នុងឆ្នាំ 2009 បន្ទាប់ពីរង់ចាំរយៈពេល 7 ឆ្នាំ។

ម្តាយរបស់ខ្ញុំ គឺជាប្រភពនៃការលើកទឹកចិត្តរបស់ខ្ញុំ។ គាត់បានបង្រៀនខ្ញុំ ឲ្យត្រូវបន្ទាបខ្លួន ត្រូវភ្លាហាន និងត្រូវគោរពមនុស្សទៅៀតៗ។ គាត់ជាចុងភៅដ៏អស្ចារ្យ ហើយមនុស្សជាច្រើននៅក្នុងសហគមន៍ បានស្រឡាញ់គាត់ និងបានគោរពការបរិច្ឆាគរបស់គាត់ ក្នុងការរក្សាវប្បធម៌ខ្មែររបស់យើង ឲ្យនៅរស់រាន។ យើងមានទំនាក់ទំនងយ៉ាងជិតដិត ប៉ុន្តែខ្ញុំបានភ្លាយជាគ្រាំគ្រាចិត្ត នៅពេលគាត់បានទទួលមរណភាពភ្លាមៗ នៅឆ្នាំក្នុងឆ្នាំ 2012។ ព្រឹទ្ធាចារ្យម្នាក់បាននិយាយនៅងមន្ទីរពេទ្យ ថា "ដំណើររបស់គាត់បានពោរពេញ ឲ្យគាត់បានទទួលមរណភាព នៅងកន្លែងបរិសុទ្ធ ជាកន្លែងដែលបេះដូង និងការប្ងូរផ្ការ់របស់គាត់ បានជើ្យសំរប់យ៉ាងជ្រៅ ចំពោះព្រះពុទ្ធ"។ នៅពេលនោះ វាគឺជាការពិបាក ទទួលយក តែនៅឥឡូវនេះខ្ញុំដឹង ថាគ្មានកន្លែងណាទៀតដែលប្រសើរជាង ដែលគាត់នឹងចង់បាន នៅពេលវេលារបស់គាត់បានមកដល់។ គាត់នឹងត្រូវបាននឹករលឹកជានិរន្ត។

ខ្ញុំចង់បន្តកេរ្តិ៍ដំណែលនៃឱពុកម្តាយរបស់ខ្ញុំ តាមការបង្កើតភូមិមួយ ពេញដោយសេចក្តីស្រឡាញ់ មួបអាហារ និងសន្តិសុខ សំរាប់កូនប្រុស របស់ខ្ញុំ ព្រមទាំងញាតិសន្តានរបស់ខ្ញុំផ្ទាល់ដែរ។ ហានៈជាកូនខ្មែរ 1.5 ជំនាន់ ខ្ញុំចង់ជួយរក្សាសហគមន៍ពុទ្ធសាសនារបស់យើង និងបង្រៀនកូន ខ្មែររក្មេងៗ កុំឲ្យខ្លាចនឹងសួរសំណួរ ថាអាធជីកនាំគេ ឆ្ពោះទៅរកការយល់ដឹងល្អប្រសើរ អំពីខ្លួនរបស់គេៗ ខ្ញុំក៏ចង់ជួយជាស់តើ្របពួកយុវវ័យ ឲ្យបន្តការអប់រំរបស់តេៗតែមទៀត និងរុករកការសិក្សាដ៏ខ្ពង់ខ្ពស់។ ជាសំខាន់បំផុត ខ្ញុំចង់ចែករំលែកតម្លៃតម្លៃទាំងនេ ថាម្តាយរបស់ខ្ញុំបានបំពាក់បំប៉នខ្ញុំ៖ ត្រូវបន្ទាបខ្លួន ត្រូវគោរពមនុស្សទៅៀតៗ និងត្រូវមានសេចក្តីក្លាហានគ្រប់គ្រប់គ្រាន់ ទើបបានល្អ។

...PROBABLY THE ONLY SOUTHEAST ASIAN IN THE ROOM THATS ON PAROLE. FACING IMMIGRATION, HOMELESSNESS, POVERTY, DRUG ADDICTION, ETC. ECT... YET. EVERYBODY IN THE ROOM IS RELATED TO INDIVIDUALS LIKE ME.

Reclaimed image courtesy of Little Laos on the Prairie.

Image courtesy of Khit Nang Vilaylack Khounbanam

NATASINH IN SAVANNAKHET

ບາກຕະສິນຢູ່ແຂວງສະຫວັນນະເຂດ

Khit Nang Vilaylack Khounbanam, 62
Minneapolis

Khit is from Savannakhet, Laos. She left Laos right before the war ended. She lives in Minneapolis with her husband KouKeo and has one son named Christopher "Keo Noy." She is a beautician and manicurist with more than 30 years doing hair design and skin care.

I was born and raised in the southern town of Savannakhet, Laos. My maiden name is Vilaylack. The Vilaylack are well known as a lineage of artists and musicians. I'm the middle child of a big family of 9 siblings, with an extended family from Vientiane down to Pakse. My father's day job was a police investigator and during the evenings and weekends, he played traditional Lao music. Most of his children were involved with music and dance.

Growing up was a warm and happy time for me as a young woman. I was taught Lao classics and how to fawn for as long as I could remember. When Friday evening came around, it was a regular sight to see the Vilaylacks jamming together. We sang and danced for many events and were the go-to family for community weddings in town. I remember fondly that part of my life as a traditional Lao girl. When the king came to visit, I had my finest Lao silk on and my hair up in a perfect bun and I fawned to songs like Lao Pan for the royal family.

I was known for having an energetic rapport with everyone around me in town, attending day and evening school, where I met my husband. I was blessed for remembering little about the war. One event I recall is that in '72, men wearing all green marched into town. That's all I remember from the war before I left. In '74, my husband got a scholarship to study in France, so we weren't there during the collapse of the country. His studies and work took us to Singapore and then we settled in Minneapolis in '83. While my husband attended graduate school I attended beauty school. I opened the first Lao-owned hair salon called "Khit Studio" in South Minneapolis on Nicollet Avenue. I have continued to work as a beautician ever since.

When I go back to Laos, I still sing and dance at our family reunions. I love singing Lao dang deum, which is like Southern Lao blues. Singing is healing for me and I hope to continue doing that with my future grandchildren.

ກິດ ບາງ ວິໄລລັກ ຂຸບບາບຳ, ອາຍຸ **62** ປີ
Minneapolis

ກິດ ເປັນຄົນແຂວງສະຫວັນນະເຂດ, ສປປ ລາວ; ແລະ ໄດ້ອົບພະຍົກອອກຈາກປະເທດ ຫຼັງຈາກທີ່ສົງຄາມໄດ້ສິ້ນສຸດລົງ. ກິດ ອາໃສຢູ່ເມືອງມິນີເອັບໂປລິສ ກັບ ສາມີຂອງເພິ່ນຊື່ ພູແກ້ວ ແລະ ມີລູກຊາຍ ນຳກັບພີ່ງຄົນຊື່ ຄິດສໂຕເຟີ "ແກ້ວບ້ອຍ." ກິດ ປະກອບອາຊີບເປັນຊ່າງເສີມສວຍ, ເຮັດຜົມ, ທຳເລັບ ແລະ ເບິ່ງແຍງຜົວພັນໃຫ້ ລູກຄ້າເປັນເວລາຫຼາຍກວ່າ 30 ປີ.

ຂ້າພະເຈົ້າເກີດ ແລະ ເຕີບໃຫຍ່ຢູ່ແຂວງສະຫວັນນະເຂດ, ປະເທດລາວ. ນາມສະກຸນຂອງຂ້າພະເຈົ້າ ກ່ອນແຕ່ງງານແມ່ນ ວິໄລລັກ, ຕະກຸນຂອງພວກເຮົາມັກ ແລະ ຮັກໃນດົນຕີ, ສຽງເພງ ແລະ ສິນລະປະ. ຂ້າພະເຈົ້າເປັນລູກຄົນກາງໃນອ້າຍເອື້ອຍນ້ອງທັງໝົດ 9 ຄົນ, ພວກເຮົາມີຍາດຕິພີ່ນ້ອງຢູ່ທັງບະຄອນ ທຸງວຽງຈັນ ແລະ ປາກເຊ. ສ່ວນພໍ່ຂອງຂ້າພະເຈົ້າປະກອບອາຊີບເປັນນາຍຕຳຫຼວດສືບສອນ ແລະ ມີອາຊີບເສີມເປັນນັກຮ້ອງ, ຮ້ອງເພງລາວດັ້ງເດີມ; ຍ້ອນແບບນັ້ນລູກໆຂອງເພິ່ນຈິ່ງມີ ສ່ວນຮ່ວມໃນດົນຕີ ແລະ ການຟ້ອນເຊິ່ງຍ່ວງກັນ.

ຂ້າພະເຈົ້າເອງເຕີບໃຫຍ່ໃນສະພາບເອດລ້ອມດີ ແລະ ອົບອຸ່ນ, ໄດ້ຮຽນຟ້ອນ ແລະ ສິນລະປະແຕ່ຍັງນ້ອຍ. ຂ້າພະເຈົ້າຍັງຈື່ໄດ້ດີ, ທຸກໆຕອນແລງຂອງວັນສຸກແມ່ນມີ້ທີ່ຄອບຄົວ ຈະພາກເຮົາຕ້ອງມາປຸ້ມລຸມກັນ ເພື່ອ ຝຶກດົນຕີ; ຖ້າມີງານສັງສັນໃນເຂດໝູ່ບ້ານ, ພວກເຮົາກໍຈະຖືກຮັບຈ້າງໄປສະແດງ. ດ້ວຍພີ່ງພວກເຮົາໄດ້ ມີໂອກາດໄປໂຊການສະແດງໃຫ້ເຈົ້າຊີວິດ ແລະ ຄອບຄົວເພິ່ນຮັບຊົມ, ຂ້າພະເຈົ້າຍັງຈື່ໄດ້ວ່າມື້ນັ້ນ, ຂ້າພະເຈົ້າເກົ້າຜົມ ແລະ ຟ້ອນເພງລາວພັນນຳດ້ວຍ.

ຂ້າພະເຈົ້າເປັນຄົນຄ່ອນຂ້າງມີຄວາມກະຕືລືລົ້ນກັບທຸກໆຢ່າງ, ເຊິ່ງຫຼາຍໆຄົນກໍເວົ້າເປັນສຽງຍ່ວງກັນ. ຂ້າພະເຈົ້າຮຽນຫັຽສິທັງພາກເຊົ້າ ແລະ ພາກແລງ ແລະ ໄດ້ພົບກັບສາມີຢູ່ໂຮງຮຽນ ຍ້ອນພວກເຮົາຮຽນ ໂຮງຮຽນຍ່ວງກັນ. ຖິວ່າໂຊກຊົຕາຫນີ້ຂ້າພະເຈົ້າຍັງບາງເທດຄາມກ່ຽວກັບສິງຄາມບໍ່ໄດ້ຢູ່. ນີ້ພີ່ງໃນຊ່ວງປີ 1972, ຂ້າພະເຈົ້າເຂົ້ນຜູ້ຊາຍຈຳບວດຫຼາຍ ໃສ່ຊຸດສິຽວເຄົບສອບສະຫນາມຢູ່ໃນເມືອງ. ຂ້າພະເຈົ້າຈື່ໄດ້ ເທົ່ານັ້ນ ແລະ ຫຼັງຈາກນັ້ນ, ປີ 1974, ສາມີຂອງຂ້າພະເຈົ້າກໍໄດ້ຖືກຮັບ ທຶນການສຶກສາເພື່ອໄປສຶກສາ ຕໍ່ຢູ່ປະເທດຝຣັ່ງເສດ, ພວກເຮົາເລີຍບໍ່ໄດ້ຢູ່ໃນຊ່ວງແຕກແຍກຂອງບ້ານເມືອງ. ທັງການສຶກສາ ແລະ ການງານຂອງສາມີຂ້າພະເຈົ້າເຮັດ ໃຫ້ພວກເຮົາໄດ້ຍ້າຍໄປຢູ່ປະເທດສິງກະໂປ ແລະ ຫຼັງຈາກນັ້ນ ກໍໄດ້ຍົກຍ້າຍມາເມືອງມິນີເອັບໂປລິສ ໃນປີ 1983. ສາມີຂອງຂ້າພະເຈົ້າໄດ້ສຶກສາປະລິນຍາໂທ ຕໍ່ ແລະ ສ່ວນຂ້າພະເຈົ້າເອງກໍໄດ້ສຶກສາດ້ານເສີມສວຍ, ເປີດຮ້ານເສີມສວຍ ແລະ ຍຶດຖືອາຊີບນີ້ຕັ້ງແຕ່ນັ້ນມາ, ຮ້ານເສີມສວຍຂ້າພະເຈົ້ານີ ຊື່ວ່າ "ກິດ ສຕູດີໂອ" ຕັ້ງຢູ່ຖະໜົນນີໂຄເລັດ, ພາກໃຕ້ຂອງ ເມືອງ ມິນີເອັບໂປລິສ,

ທຸກໆຄັ້ງທີ່ຂ້າພະເຈົ້າໄດ້ກັບໄປປະເທດລາວ, ຂ້າພະເຈົ້າພ້ອມຕອບຖືອກໍຈະປຸ້ມລຸມກັບເພື່ອມາຟ້ອນ ແລະ ຮ້ອງເພງ. ຂ້າພະເຈົ້າມັກທີ່ສຸດແມ່ນຮ້ອງເພງລາວດັ້ງເດີມ, ການຮ້ອງເພງແມ່ນການຜ່ອນຄາຍອັນພີ່ງ ແລະ ຂ້າພະເຈົ້າຕັ້ງໃຈຈະຮ້ອງເພງໄປເລື້ອຍໆ ແລະ ໂດຍສະເພາະລູກຫຼານຂອງຂ້າພະເຈົ້າ.

2018

Announced my candidacy to run for office for Ramsey County commissioner District 3. Running for equity for all & to reflect our SEA community so that we thrive

Image by Thaiphy Phan-Quang

Image by Thaiphy Phan-Quang

I COME FROM A VILLAGE OF FLOWERS

Tôi xuất thân từ một làng có nhiều hoa

Huỳnh Thị Lành, 77
Saint Paul

I was born in the beautiful city of Saigon, the pearl of Southeast Asia at the time. Life was simple for me. Everyday I would wake up, go to the store and buy food for my family. My father and mother would leave early in the morning, so I would take care of the household and work with the helpers to make sure my nine siblings were fed and ready for the day. I spent most of my time studying. Outside of my family and schooling responsibilities, I would watch the cinema. Studying French, I loved the romance films. I remember watching films with famous actresses like Audrey Hepburn and Marilyn Monroe. As a teenager I worked in a French-owned factory, making oxygen tanks.

After getting married in 1965, I moved to Go Vap, a suburb of Saigon. Go Vap in my memory was full of flower villages specializing in delivering fresh flowers to Saigon for holidays and New Year celebrations, bustling with busy restaurants. Leaving this place, I would always remember streets jam-packed with motorcycles, beautiful clothing and smells of grilled meat wafting in the air.

Before the war began, I had no idea what was happening outside of the village I was in. I lived away from all the fighting. However, this all changed in the year 1968. I heard in the Việt Namese newspaper that the city of Hue began fighting and there was civil unrest. The next year, the fighting came to my city. As I lived close to the South Việt Nam barracks, I recall the Communist soldiers on the roof of my house shooting down to the artillery barrack next to my house, while US airplanes dropped rockets from the sky. One memory that still extremely frightens me is when soldiers lined hordes of dead bodies out on the street as a warning sign. I fled with only the clothes on my back.

Life afterwards was hard, there was often no food. All of our money in the bank was taken and my income drastically dropped. The rations that were given to our large family were hardly enough to survive. When food became scarce, my family and I would just eat rice and potatoes. We struggled, so when the opportunity to go to the US came, we grasped it. My parents and siblings went first, around 1984.

But when they attempted to sponsor me, the paperwork took a very long time. When I got the chance in 2004, my children had already been raising families of their own. So I immigrated alone.

My first year in America was horrible. I missed everything about my home country, my family and the life I had back then. I would sleep in a cold basement every night, shivering. I longed the ability to go where I wanted, to be self determined and not rely so much on others. I struggle with depression, from all the tribulations and challenges I faced during my life. But I still have faith that there is better to come. If you can help, help without asking anything in return. If I am able to make other people happy, I am happy. Have faith that you'll be taken care of in return. You must believe.

——

Huỳnh Thị Lành, 77
Saint Paul

Tôi sinh ra tại thành phố Sài Gòn tươi đẹp, hòn ngọc viễn đông lúc bấy giờ của Đông Nam Á. Cuộc sống của tôi khá đơn giản. Mỗi sáng thức dậy, tôi ra chợ mua thức ăn về cho gia đình. Cha mẹ tôi thường thức dậy sớm để đi làm. Tôi giúp cha mẹ chăm sóc chín đứa em, cắt đặt công việc nhà với người giúp việc để sửa soạn cho những hoạt động của chúng trong ngày. Tôi giành phần lớn thời gian của mình để học. Khi hoàn tất việc học và những nghĩa vụ trong gia đình, tôi thích xem phim. Do học tiếng Pháp, tôi rất thích những phim tình cảm lãng mạn. Tôi nhớ mình đã từng xem những bộ phim với các diễn viên nổi tiếng như Audrey Hepburn và Marilyn Monroe. Khi đến tuổi thành niên, tôi làm việc cho một nhà máy sản xuất bình ốc-xi của Pháp.

Sau khi lập gia đình vào năm 1965, tôi chuyển đến sống ở Gò Vấp, một quận vùng ven Sài Gòn. Lúc bấy giờ Gò Vấp theo trí nhớ của tôi còn rất nhiều làng hoa chuyên cung cấp hoa tươi cho Sài Gòn trong những dịp lễ tết, xen lẫn các hàng quán nhộn nhịp. Khi rời đi khỏi nơi đó, tôi lúc nào cũng nhớ đến những con đường đầy ngập xe gắn máy, những dãy bán quần áo đẹp và mùi thơm của thịt nướng hoà quyện trong không khí.

Trước khi chiến tranh nổ ra, tôi hoàn toàn không biết điều gì đang diễn ra bên ngoài khu xóm mình đang ở. Tôi ở một nơi xa khỏi những trận chiến. Tuy nhiên, mọi việc thay đổi vào năm 1968. Tôi xem trên báo thấy thành phố Huế bắt đầu có

chiến tranh và những cuộc đàn áp công dân. Năm sau đó, chiến tranh bắt đầu lan đến nơi tôi ở. Vì ở ngay cạnh doanh trại Việt Nam Cộng Hòa, tôi không thể quên những lúc lính Việt Cộng bắn tỉa trên mái nhà của tôi xuống trại pháo binh sát cạnh nhà, trong khi máy bay Mỹ bắn Rocket xuống từ trên trời. Một ký ức hãi hùng mà tôi vẫn còn nhớ đó là khi lính rải hàng đống xác người khắp trên đường để cảnh cáo. Tôi chạy trốn với chỉ mỗi quần áo trên người.

Cuộc sống những năm sau đó trở nên rất khó khăn và thường xuyên chịu nhiều đói khát. Tiền bạc trong ngân hàng bị mất hết, đồng lương rớt từ cao xuống thấp. Lương thực được phân phát cho gia đình lớn của tôi không đủ để sống. Khi lương thực trở nên hiếm hoi, tôi và gia đình chỉ ăn cơm trắng với khoai mì. Vì cả nhà vật và để tồn tại nên khi có cơ hội đi Mỹ, tôi lập tức nắm lấy. Cha mẹ tôi và các anh chị em đi trước, vào năm 1984. Nhưng khi gia đình bảo lãnh tôi thì làm giấy tờ mất thời gian rất lâu. Khi cơ hội của tôi đến vào năm 2004 thì các con của tôi đã lớn và có gia đình của riêng mình nên tôi di dân một mình sang Mỹ.

Năm đầu tiên ở Mỹ đối với tôi thật kinh hoàng. Tôi nhớ mọi thứ ở quê nhà, gia đình và cuộc sống của mình trước đây. Tôi ngủ co ro dưới tầng hầm lạnh giá mỗi đêm. Tôi ước mong được đi đến nơi mà tôi muốn, được tự lập và không phải phụ thuộc vào người khác. Tôi chiến đấu với bệnh trầm cảm vì những khó khăn khổ cực tôi đã trải qua trong cuộc sống. Nhưng tôi vẫn tin rằng những điều tốt đẹp sẽ đến. "Nếu bạn có thể giúp, giúp mà không cần đòi hỏi gì cho mình. Nếu tôi có thể làm cho người khác hạnh phúc, tôi sẽ cảm thấy hạnh phúc. Hãy có đức tin là bạn sẽ được bù đắp và chăm sóc lại. Bạn phải có niềm tin."

"When eating the fruit, remember
who planted the tree."

Việt Proverb

Image courtesy of Pa Houa Chang

SPEAKING AMERICA

Hais Lus Ameslikas

Pa Houa Chang, 22
Minneapolis

My dad was in General Vang Pao's CIA army. In 1975, he had the opportunity to leave with Vang Pao to America right after the war, but stayed back. When all the refugee camps closed, my parents and older siblings, like many other Hmong people, moved to Wat Tham Krabok to seek sanctuary.

When I was little, I played all day with the other wat kids. We weren't old enough to go to school so we would just recreationally roam around the temple grounds. I remember us climbing the tombstones in the graveyard where they had buried Hmong people who passed away. We were kids so we didn't know any better. Whenever it rained, all the kids would come out, sometimes wearing nothing at all, and we danced and played in the rain together. That's my favorite memory of Wat Tham Krabok.

My parents ran a shop outside of our house. They sold general merchandise to the other wat residents. There were many people who set up various shops outside their homes or the market so they could make money. In 2005, we were finally sponsored by my older brother and able to come to the United States. I was only six years old. I was so excited to ride on a plane for the first time. We arrived in Detroit, Michigan. I still remember seeing snow for the first time!

When I started school in America it was really difficult. I didn't speak English and I remember having an interpreter with me at all times. In the beginning I was frustrated because I didn't know how to tell my teacher when I needed to use the restroom. I would just wait until there was free time to go. We were bullied often at school, and couldn't communicate what happened. One time a girl in my class stole my silver dollar coin that my parents gave me. I was so upset, but what could I do? That day after school I told my mom what happened. She told me to forget about it because there was nothing we could do.

Growing up in America, home life was difficult. As we got better at English we began translating for our parents. My dad was really strict about what my sisters and I could do outside the house, so my older sister wasn't able to do much except go to school and come back home. When I became older I really wanted to join after school clubs but it was difficult to explain to my parents what I wanted. They would assume I was out doing bad things. I didn't let the things my parents said stop me though. They were just looking out for me, but didn't know how else to communicate that. I'm glad I persisted despite their disapproval. In middle school I rode the city bus on my own so I could take extra credit classes in preparation for high school. At first, I got lost in the city, but eventually I figured out how to ride the bus and go places by myself.

If I could give advice to my younger self I would say, "Don't be afraid and speak up more!" I'm proud of how far I've come. I honestly didn't realize it until now, but I've accomplished a lot. One of my goals growing up was to know English fluently, and I'm glad I worked hard to achieve that.

Paj Huab Tsab, 22
Minneapolis

Kuv txiv yog Nai Phoo Vaj Pov ib tug CIA (Central Intelligence Agency) tub rog. Nyob rau xyoo 1975, thaum Nai Phoo Vaj Pov thiab CIA tau swb tsov rog, kuv txiv tau muaj lub hwv tsam uas nrog Nai Phoo Vaj Pov ya tawm teb chaws Nplog mus rau Meskas, tiam sis nws txiav txim siab tsis mus. Thaum cov Yeej Thoj Nam Tawg Rog raug kaw tag lawm, li lwm cov neeg Hmoob uas tseem nyob, kuv tsev neeg lawv tau mus nyob rau hauv zos Vaj Loog Tsua. Vaj Loog Tsua yog peb Hmoob lub chaw nkaum thiab lub chaw nyab xeeb.

Thaum kuv tseem me, kuv yeej niaj hnub uasi nrog lwm cov me nyuam yaus uas nyob hauv zos Vaj Loog Tsua. Peb kuj tsis tau loj txaus uas yuav mus kawm ntawv tau. Vim li ntawv, peb ces tsuas mus nrhiav kev lom zem rau tim vav xwb. Kuv tseem nco tau thaum peb mus nce cov lag zeb nyob saum cov ntxa uas lawv faus faus neeg tuag. Vim peb yog me nyuam yaus xwb, peb tsis paub tab dab tsi li. Yog thaum twg ntuj los nag, txhua tus me nyuam yaus ces yeej tawm tuaj nyob nraum zoov. Tej thaum ces liab qab tawm tuaj xwb. Tiam sis txawm li cas los peb sawv daws kuj tuaj lom zem, seev cev, thiab ua si ua ke. Ntawv yog qhov uas kuv nco tshaj plaws nyob rau hauv zos Vaj Loog Tsua.

Kuv niam thiab kuv txiv nkawv tau ua ib lub tab laj sab nraum peb lub tsev. Nkawv kuj muag khoom uas neeg niaj hnub siv rau cov pej xeem uas nyob hauv Wat Tham Krabok. Kuj muaj coob leej ntau tus neeg uas tau ua tab laj sab raum lawv tsev losis rau tom kiab tom khw, vim ua tab laj yog ib txoj kev nrhiav noj nrhiav haus. Nyob rau xyoo 2004, kuv niam tus niam laus tau ua ntaub ntawv los tos peb mus nyob rau Mes Kas. Thaum ntawv kuv nyuam qhuav muaj rau xyoo xwb. Kuv muaj siab thiab zoo siab tshaj plaws li, vim kuv yuav tau mus caij dav hlau thawj thawj zaug nyob rau hauv kuv lub neej. Peb tuaj poob rau hauv Detroit, Michigan. Kuv tseem nco tau thawj zaug uas kuv pom daus!

Thaum kuv nyuam qhuav pib kawm ntawv nyob rau Meskas teb, nws nyuab heev li. Kuv tsis paub lus Askiv. Kuv tseem nco tau hais tias yeej muaj ib tug neeg txhais lus nrog nraim kuv tas li. Thaum xub thawj kuv meem txom heev, vim kuv tsis paub yuav qhia tus xib fwb hais tias kuv xav mus siv chav dej. Kuv ces yeej tos thaum muaj sij hawm ua si ces kuv mam mus xwb. Peb yeej raug luag saib tsis taus ntau zaus tom tsev kawm ntawv, tiam sis peb ho tsis paub yuav piav rau lawv li cas thiab. Muaj ib zaug, ib tug me nyuam ntxhais nyob rau hauv hoob tau nyiag kuv lub nyiaj duas dawb, uas yog kuv niam kuv txiv muab rau kuv. Kuv tau chim siab heev, tiam sis kuv yuav ua tau dab tsi? Thaum kuv los txog tsev kuv tau los qhia kuv niam. Kuv niam tsuas hais tias kom kav liam lawm xwb, vim peb yeej ua tsis tau dab tsi.

Tuaj loj hlob rau lub teb chaws Meskas no, lub neej nyob hauv tsev nyuab kawg li. Thaum peb txawj hais thiab to taub lus Askiv zog lawm ces, peb tau los pib txhais lus rau kuv niam thiab kuv txiv nkawv. Kuv txiv tau coj nruj heev rau kuv thiab kuv cov viv ncaus peb, thaum peb yuav tawm mus ua ib qho num tawm ntawm peb lub tsev. Vim li ntawv, kuv cov viv ncaus ces tsuas yog mus kawm ntawv rov qab los tsev xwb. Thaum kuv muaj hnub nyug zog lawm, kuv tau xav mus tsev kawm ntawv cov clubs, tiam sis kuv yuav qhia kuv niam kuv txiv nkawv txog qhov kuv xav ua mas nws nyuab heev li. Nkawv yuav xav hais tias tej zaum yog kuv tawm rooj ces kuv yuav mus ua tej yam tsis zoo xwb. Tab sis kuv yeej tsis cia nkawv cov lus los cheem kuv thiab. Kuv yeej paub hais tias nkawv tsuas xav qhov zoo rau kuv xwb, tab sis nkawv tsis paub yuav qhia qhov ntawv li cas rau kuv xwb. Kuv zoo siab kawg uas kuv kuj peem tiag txawm tias kuv niam thiab kuv txiv nkawv tsis pom zoo. Thaum kuv nyob Middle School kuv ib leeg los kuv yeej caij npav, tsuav kom kuv tau mus kawm hoob ntxiv kom kuv npaj tau zoo ua ntej kuv yuav mus High School xwb. Thawj thawj zaug uas kuv caij npav, kuv tau mus poob zoo rau hauv nroog loj, tab sis caij ntev mus ces kuv kuj to taub thiab paub caij lawm thiab. Kuv ib leeg xwb los kuv yeej caij tau mus ub mus no lawm.

Yog kuv qhia tau ib lo lus rau kuv tus kheej thaum kuv tseem hluas, kuv yuav qhia hais tias: "Tsis txhob ntshai thiab yuav tsum tawm suab ntxiv!" Kuv zoo siab thiab qhuas kuv tus kheej qhov kuv tau los txog deb npaum li no. Qhov tseeb tiag, tam sim no kuv nyuam qhuav ras tau hais tias kuv yeej tau ua tiav ntau yam heev li lawm. Thaum kuv loj hlob, kuv ib lub hom phiaj yog kuv xav paub thiab hais lus Askiv kom meej. Kuv zoo siab uas kuv tau sib zog peem heev kuv thiaj li to taub thiab hais lus Askiv meej lawm.

COme HoMe

8 Responses to the Phrase, Go Back to Where You Came From

By Kevin Yang

1.
Oh,
you mean,
Minnesota?
In which case,
here I am.

2.
Oh,
you mean,
where I'm really from.
In which case,
here I am.

3.
If this is in reference
to my ancestors,
then
you are going to have to be
a little bit more specific.
How about trying,
"Go back to St. Paul",
"Go back to Fresno"
"Go back to Ban Vinai"
"Go back to Long Cheng"
"Go back to Xieng Khuong"
"Go back to Ghuizhou"
Upon taking my advice,
also realize,
you are not the first
to give the command of
return,
to point us
in the opposite direction
with the barrel of a pistol,
to deny us
the ability to claim our soil
as anything else but ours.
Call me Hmong,
before you call me American
because Hmong is the closest word
I know to home.

4.

Do you ever wonder where you came from?
Do you ever find comfort,
in vague memories of Ellis Island?
How many servings
from the melting pot
did it take for you to arrive
at this conversation?
Maybe,
you take pride in the May Flower.
Maybe,
you are an original American.
Do you ever ask yourself
if the land that you stand on,
once belonged to someone else?
Do you ever ask yourself
if,
maybe,
the land
never belonged to any of us
and if instead,
we belonged to the land?

5.

In the winter of 2013,
I made the journey back
to Thailand,
hoping to find
our villages still dotting
the slopes of mountainsides,
imagining,
kwv txhiaj would be heard
echoing through the valleys.
Upon entering the house of an elder,
he apologizes to me,
embarrassed that his youngest son
could not introduce himself to me in our language,
tells me,
that if you want to grow up
to be anything more than a farmer or a servant
in this country,
you must learn to leave your language behind.
I want to tell him,
that throughout my time here,
I have never felt
so close to home

6.

My mother tells me,
that before
I ever took in my first breath,
I was an invisible spirit
floating around the clouds
waiting for a stomach
that could paint me pink.
My mother tells me,
that death is a journey home,
death is a slow walk back,
that if not done carefully
our spirit will wander lost
cursing those still living,
but under the watchful eyes
of our loved ones,
we always find our way.

7.

For most of my life,
I was convinced
that the hummingbird
did not possess a pair of feet,
instead always existing
in a state of mid-flight.
How sad,
I thought,
to always be at the mercy of the wind,
to be so close to the earth
yet own none of it.
My time here has taught me,
how lucky,
the hummingbird,
to belong to the sky.

8.

I am going.
I am going.

KHMER FREEDOM FIGHTER

អ្នកច្បាំងរកសេរីភាពខ្មែរ

*Hun H. & You H.
Saint Paul

My name is Hun. I am a soldier, thus I am a freedom fighter. I grew up in Siem Reap, Cambodia. My childhood memories were filled with joyful times. Everyone in the village shared and bond through community meals and we cared for one another. It was a small village with peaceful scenery of Angkor Wat. Before I enlisted in the army, I was a monk at the nearby temple. During the war, I went to three training camps. I lived in Việt Nam for two years and spent another two years in Thailand. Fortunately, I used a deceased soldier's name during my time in the army. So I was able to flee the country and be reunited with my wife.

Then I came to Minnesota in 1979. We settled in Edina and moved to Saint Paul in 1985. My first job was at the Radisson Hotel and then I got a job at a donut shop. My salary was $3.10/per hour. I have three sons and am currently retired.

My name is You H. I am a wife of soldiers and my life is filled with worry. I married my first husband who died during the war. My second husband is Hun H., and he is also a soldier who enter into the army during the war. I grew up in Siem Reap, Cambodia. I was 19 years old when I wed my husband, Hun. It wasn't love at first sight nor a romantic love story. It was an arranged marriage. Hun had fallen in love with me and asked my parents for my hand in marriage. He contributed 3,000 Thai Baht to help pay for the wedding. Then we wed soon after he visited me.

In 1979, we fled our country and arrived in Minnesota. We both went to school and attended church. I later gave birth to our first son and settled in Saint Paul. It was our toughest time. I remember crying and feeling frustrated that I wasn't able to speak English. We were in a large country and I wasn't adjusting to the new way of living.

I missed my simple life in Siem Reap. Before the war, I was a student and a daughter. My country had prosperity and life was simple and authentic. My advice for the next generation is to love and respect one another.

---

*ហៀន ហ. & យូ ហ.
Saint Paul

ខ្ញុំឈ្មោះហៀន។ ខ្ញុំជាទាហានម្នាក់ ម្លោះហើយខ្ញុំជាអ្នកច្បាំងរកសេរីភាព។ ខ្ញុំបានធំធាត់នៅក្នុងខេត្រសៀមរាប កម្ពុជា។ អនុស្សាវរីយ៍នៃ កុមារភាពរបស់ខ្ញុំ បានពោរពេញទៅដោយពេលអរសប្បាយ។ គ្រប់ៗគ្នានៅក្នុងភូមិ បានចែកចាយម្ហូបអាហាររគ្នា ហើយក៏ស្ថិតស្ថលនឹងគ្នា នៅសហទំាងសហគមន៍ ហើយយើងបានយកចិត្តទុកដាក់នឹងគ្នា។ វាគឺជាភូមិមួយតូច ដោយមានទស្សនីយភាពដ៏សន្តិភាពនៃអង្គរវត្ត។ នៅមុនពេលខ្ញុំចុះឈ្មោះចូលធ្វើយោធា ខ្ញុំគឺលោកសង្ឃមួយអង្គ នៅវត្តក្បែរខ្ញុំ។ នៅក្នុងអំឡុងពេលសង្គ្រាម ខ្ញុំបានទៅជំរំហ្វឹកហ្វឺនបីកន្លែង។ ខ្ញុំបានរស់នៅក្នុងប្រទេសវៀតណាម ចំនួនពីរឆ្នាំ និងបានចំណាយពេលពីរឆ្នាំទៀត នៅប្រទេសថៃ។ ជាក់ស្ដែងសំណាងល្អ ខ្ញុំបានប្រើឈ្មោះ របស់ទាហានម្នាក់ដែលបានស្លាប់ ក្នុងអំឡុងពេលខ្ញុំនៅក្នុងជួរយោធា។ ដូច្នេះហើយ ខ្ញុំអាចភៀសខ្លួនចេញពីប្រទេសបាន និងបានជួបជុំជាមួយប្រពន្ធរបស់ខ្ញុំវិញ។

ជាបន្ទាប់មក ខ្ញុំក៏បានមកដល់រដ្ឋ Minnesota ក្នុងឆ្នាំ 1979។ ខ្ញុំបានតាំងលំនៅក្នុងក្រុង Edina និងបានផ្លាស់ទៅក្រុង Saint Paul ក្នុងឆ្នាំ 1985។ ការងារដំបូងរបស់ខ្ញុំគឺនៅសណ្ឋាគារ Radisson និងបន្ទាប់មកទៀត ខ្ញុំបានការងារមួយនៅហាងលក់នំដូណាត់។ រវិប្រាក់ឈ្នួលរបស់ខ្ញុំនៅពេលនោះ គឺមួយម៉ោង $3.10។ ខ្ញុំមានកូនប្រុសបីនាក់ និងនៅបច្ចុប្បន្ននេះ ខ្ញុំបានចូលនិវត្តន៍ហើយ។

ខ្ញុំឈ្មោះ យូ ហុម។ ខ្ញុំជាភរិយានៃទាហាន ហើយជីវិតរបស់ខ្ញុំ បានពោរពេញទៅដោយសេចក្ដីព្រួយបារម្ភ។ ខ្ញុំបានរៀបអាពាហ៍ពិពាហ៍នឹងស្វាមីដំបូងរបស់ខ្ញុំ ដែលបានទទួលមរណភាពក្នុងអំឡុងពេលសង្គ្រាម។ ស្វាមីទីពីររបស់ខ្ញុំ គឺឈ្មោះហៀន ហុម ហើយគាត់ក៏ជាទាហានដែរ ដែលបានចូលក្នុងជួរយោធា ក្នុងអំឡុងពេលសង្គ្រាម។ ខ្ញុំបានធំធាត់នៅក្នុងខេត្រសៀមរាប កម្ពុជា។ ខ្ញុំមានអាយុ 19 ឆ្នាំ នៅពេលខ្ញុំបានរៀបការនឹងស្វាមីរបស់ខ្ញុំ ឈ្មោះហៀន។ នៅពេលបានឃើញដំបូង

ខ្ញុំមិនបានស្រឡាញ់ទេ ឬក៏គ្មានរឿងស្នេហាដែលវង្វេងចិត្តឡើយ។ វាគឺជាអាពាហ៍ពិពាហ៍ដែលបានផ្សំផ្គុំ។ ហេីុនបានធ្លាក់ក្នុងសេចក្តីស្នេហា ជាមួយនឹងខ្ញុំ និងក៏បានសូមឩពុកម្តាយរបស់ខ្ញុំ ដេីម្បីចាប់ដៃខ្ញុំរៀបអាពាហ៍ពិពាហ៍។ គាត់បានបរិច្ចាគប្រាក់ថៃ ចំនួន 3,000 បាត ដេីម្បីជួយបង់ថ្លៃនៃការរៀបការ។ ជាបន្ទាប់មក យេីងក៏បានរៀបការធាប់ៗ បន្ទាប់ពីគាត់បានជូបខ្ញុំ។

នៅក្នុងឆ្នាំ 1979 យេីងបានភៀសខ្លួនចេញពីប្រទេសរបស់យេីង និងបានមកដល់រដ្ឋ Minnesota។ យេីងទាំងពីរនាក់ បានទៅសាលា និងបានទៅព្រះវិហារ។ នៅពេលក្រោយមក ខ្ញុំក៏បានឡ្បកំណេីតកូនប្រុសដំបូងរបស់យេីង និងបានតាំងលំនៅក្នុងក្រុង Saint Paul។ វាគឺជាពេលវេលាដ៏លំបាកបំផុត របស់យេីង។ ខ្ញុំបាននឹកចាំពីការយំ និងការមានអារម្មណ៍អន្ទះអន្ទែង ដែលខ្ញុំមិនអាចនិយាយភាសាអង់គ្លេសបាន។ យេីងនៅក្នុងប្រទេសមួយដ៏ចំ ហេីយខ្ញុំក៏មិនបានសំរបសំរួលខ្លួន ទៅនឹងជីវភាពរស់នៅថ្មី។

ខ្ញុំបាននឹកពីជីវិតស្រួលរបស់ខ្ញុំ នៅក្នុងខេត្រសៀមរាប។ នៅមុនពេលសង្គ្រាម ខ្ញុំគឺជាសិស្សម្នាក់ និងជាកូនស្រីម្នាក់។ ប្រទេសរបស់ខ្ញុំមានវិបុលភាព ហេីយជីវិតក៏ស្រួល និងទៀងទាត់។ ឪពុករបស់ខ្ញុំ សំរាប់មនុស្សជំនាន់ក្រោយ គឺត្រូវស្រឡាញ់គ្នា និងគោរពគ្នាទៅវិញទៅមក។

"If you want to be big, act small;
if you want to be tall, act short;
if you want something, offer
payment; if you want to be
knowledgeable, study; if you
want enlightenment, be virtuous;
if you want a life of ease,
overcome your difficulties."

Khmer Proverb

Image by Angelina Trâm Nguyễn

XIN CHÀO

Xin Chào

Nguyễn Minh Phan, 66
Saint Paul

I grew up in Vinh Phu, a village with 1,000 people, nested on the coast of Nghe Anh province. It was an agricultural village and the harvest would bring corn, yams, and potatoes. Under French colonialism, my entire village converted to Catholicism.

I remember being a happy child, holding both good and bad memories. My father died in the war with the French. Then, my oldest brother died when his plane crashed in Da Nang during the North-South War. I knew my mother struggled as a widow and grieving mother, raising her three remaining children in the midst of war.

When we migrated from Vinh Phu to Phan Thiet, my mother leveraged her farming knowledge to become a rice merchant, which provided enough for her family. My second oldest sibling became a Catholic priest. My third oldest sibling became a primary school teacher. Inspired by my siblings, I joined seminary school to become a priest. While in seminary school, I taught high school students chemistry, math, english, and philosophy.

After the end of the North-South War, a new regimen emerged and placed restrictions on my to path continue college or become a priest. I was sent to re-education camp twice. In re-education camp, I learned that forced starvation is an effective tactic for silencing dissenting ideas. I remember prisoners who had not eaten for days, officials at the camp served them noodles with sand thrown into it to see if people were hungry enough to eat.

I was finally able to escape by boat and ended up in Brunei, Malaysia and was sponsored by St. Columba church in 1978.

My first years were difficult and isolating. My sponsor family helped me with housing, food, and navigating my first few months in St. Paul. After that, I was on my own. At night, I remembered what I missed about Việt Nam. I was homesick. What kept me going was thinking about how I could engage in activities at school and really start to make a life for myself here. I was determined to both work and go to school.

I graduated from Saint Paul College then studied at Metropolitan State University, University of Minnesota (U of M), National College, and St. Thomas. I never graduated but cherished the knowledge I gained from my experience at those schools. I remember trying to heal my homesickness by approaching anyone on campus that looked like me. I made friends with one Chinese and one Japanese student at the U of M. On both occasions, I greeted them with, "Are you Việt?" They said no. They were as alone as I was.

Then, I found Nguyễn Thi Thanh, my lifelong sweetheart. I helped her settle into her life in St. Paul. We were both in choir together. She kept showing pictures of her old boyfriend in Seattle until that photo eventually went away. We now own a small bread shop in Saint Paul, have raised three kids together— Kim, Lam, Hoa— and are now grandparents to a child named after Stokely Carmichael.

Image by Thaiphy Phan-Quang

I remember the lonely, homesick feeling watching my mother's first years in Minnesota. My mother once told me that, after she died, she wanted her body buried in Việt Nam so her spirit would raise up from soil where people spoke her language.

The challenges of translating my life in Việt Nam to my life in Minnesota has made difficult the continuity of healing practices from one generation to the next, like understanding the power of plant medicine. All of the plants that my people knew and use to create medicine from are not grown here. For a while there was one person in Minnesota I knew that had deep experience in creating healing elixirs. I remember traveling from St. Paul to South Minneapolis to visit with Bac Truong Thanh and share ailments with him. Bac Truong Thanh would wrap bundles of his carefully curated herbs with butcher paper and twine. I would bring the bundle to ailing people, boil it up, and serve it. Bac Truong Thanh, our last Việt herb specialist died over ten years ago. Now, I must order our plant medicine from out of state or from China. In Minnesota, I feel a sense of loss not knowing who else holds Việt people's knowledge on how to heal our ailments through plant medicine. I don't see younger generations wanting to learn it. I hope they do.

Another practice I also hope the next generation will carry on is the value of Xin Chào, a humble welcome and invitation into life with each other. I hope the next generation will continue to look out for other Việt people, like family. I hope my labor on this land brings the possibility of more Việt people opening the invitation to be called on by each other when needed.

Nguyễn Minh Phan, 66
Saint Paul

Tôi lớn lên tại Vĩnh Phú, một ngôi làng với 1000 người, nằm náu mình trên bờ biển của tỉnh Nghệ An. Đây là một làng nông thu hoạch các loại ngũ cốc như bắp và khoai. Dưới thời Pháp thuộc, cả làng chuyển sang theo đạo Công giáo.

Tôi nhớ thời nhỏ mình là một đứa trẻ khá hạnh phúc với những ký ức tốt đẹp xen lẫn đau buồn. Cha tôi mất trong cuộc chiến tranh chống Pháp và sau đó anh cả cũng mất khi lái máy bay chiến đấu ở Đà Nẵng trong cuộc nội chiến Nam-Bắc. Tôi biết mẹ mình, một quả phụ vẫn đau buồn vì cái chết của chồng con, vất và nuôi ba đứa con còn lại giữa lòng chiến tranh.

Khi gia đình chuyển từ Vĩnh Phú xuống Phan Thiết, mẹ tôi dùng kiến thức về trồng trọt của mình để trở thành một thương nhân buôn bán gạo, cung cấp vừa đủ lương thực và sự an toàn cho gia đình. Người anh kế của tôi trở thành một cha xứ Công giáo và người anh chị kế đó trở thành một giáo viên tiểu học. Theo gương các anh chị mình, tôi cũng đi vào trường giòng để trở thành linh mục. Trong thời gian này, tôi dạy học sinh Trung học các môn Hóa học, Toán, Anh văn và Triết học.

Sau khi kết thúc chiến tranh Nam – Bắc, chế độ cai trị mới hình thành và cản trở con đường học lên Đại học và trở thành linh mục của tôi. Tôi bị đưa vào trại cải tạo hai lần. Ở trại cải tạo, tôi nhận ra rằng bỏ đói là một thủ thuật hiệu quả để bịt miệng những ý kiến chống đối. Khi các tù nhân bị bỏ đói nhiều ngày liên tục, các cán bộ ở trại cho họ ăn mì trộn cát để xem mọi người có đủ đói để ăn hay không. Cuối cùng, tôi thoát đi bằng con đường vượt biên, cập bến ở Brunei, Mã Lai và sau được Nhà thờ Saint Columba bảo lãnh sang Mỹ vào năm 1977.

Những năm đầu tại Mỹ Quốc thật khó khăn và cô lập. Gia đình bảo lãnh giúp tôi tìm nhà, thức ăn và hỗ trợ tôi đường đi nước bước trong những tháng đầu ở tại Saint Paul. Nhưng ngay sau đó, tôi một thân một mình. Về đêm, tôi nhớ quê nhà. Điều giúp tôi vượt qua là nghĩ đến làm cách nào để tham gia các hoạt động ở trường và thật sự bắt đầu làm lại một cuộc sống mới cho riêng mình tại đây. Tôi quyết tâm vừa đi học vừa đi làm.

Tôi tốt nghiệp cao đẳng ở Saint Paul College rồi học lên

Đại học ở các trường đại học lớn như Metropolitan State, University of Minnesota-Twin Cities, National College, và Saint Thomas. Mặc dù không tốt nghiệp nhưng tôi trân trọng những kiến thức mà mình học được ở các trường này. Tôi nhớ lại những năm này, mỗi khi nhớ nhà quá, tôi cứ thấy ai nhìn giống mình thì lại lân la đến làm quen. Tôi làm bạn với một sinh viên người Trung Quốc và một sinh viên người Nhật. Cả hai lần, tôi chào họ với câu hỏi "Anh có phải là người Việt?". Họ nói không. Họ cũng đơn độc như tôi vậy.

Sau này, tôi tìm được Nguyễn Thị Thanh, người yêu suốt đời của mình. Tôi giúp cô ấy ổn định cuộc sống ở Saint Paul vì chúng tôi cùng trong ca đoàn của nhà thờ. Cô ấy lúc đầu thường xòe hình bạn trai cũ của mình lúc ở Seattle nhưng rồi dần dần tấm hình lặng lẽ ra đi. Chúng tôi ngày nay là chủ một tiệm bánh mì nhỏ ở Saint Paul, cùng nuôi dạy ba đứa con và rồi trở thành ông bà của một cháu trai được đặt theo tên của Stokely Carmichael.

Tôi cảm nhận được sự cô đơn và nhớ nhà mỗi lần nghĩ đến những năm đầu tại Minnesota của mẹ mình. Mẹ tôi từng bảo rằng khi bà mất, bà muốn được đem xác về chôn ở Việt Nam nơi quê cha đất tổ, nơi mà mọi người nói chuyện bằng tiếng mẹ đẻ của bà để linh hồn bà được an vui.

Những khó khăn thử thách khi rời Việt Nam đến định cư ở Minnesota làm gián đoạn việc lưu truyền cho các thế hệ sau những phương pháp chữa lành truyền thống bằng cây lá. Ở đây không có những cây cỏ mà dân tộc của tôi thường dùng làm dược liệu để chữa bệnh. Trong một thời gian dài, chỉ có duy nhất một người Việt ở Minnesota biết cách dùng cây cỏ để chế biến thành dược liệu. Tôi còn nhớ những lần đi từ Saint Paul sang phía Nam Minneapolis để thăm anh Trường Thành và nhờ chữa bệnh. Anh Trường Thành cẩn thận gói những nắm dược thảo mà anh tự làm từ cây cỏ vào những miếng giấy và bó lại. Tôi đem những gói thuốc này đến cho những người bệnh, nấu sôi nhiều lần cho sắc lại và cho họ uống. Anh Trường Thành, người thầy thuốc Nam cuối cùng của người Việt tại Minnesota đã mất đi cách đây hơn 10 năm. Giờ đây, khi cần thuốc, tôi phải đặt mua từ các tiểu bang khác hoặc từ Trung Quốc. Ở Minnesota, tôi cảm nhận được sự mất mát to lớn khi không còn người Việt nào còn giữ những kiến thức về sử dụng thảo dược để trị bệnh. Nhất là khi tôi không thấy có người trẻ nào của thế hệ đi sau muốn học hỏi về lĩnh vực này mặc dù tôi rất hi vọng vào điều đó.

Một điều nữa mà tôi mong muốn cho thế hệ sau là tiếp tục

duy trì giá trị của lời chào. Một câu nói "Xin chào" để khiêm tốn chào đón và mời gọi người khác vào cuộc đời của mình, và của lẫn nhau. Tôi hi vọng rằng thế hệ sau tôi sẽ tiếp tục chăm lo cho những người Việt khác như trong một gia đình. Mong sao cho công sức của tôi trên mảnh đất này gieo cơ hội cho nhiều người Việt nữa cùng nương tựa nhau khi cần.

Image courtesy of Nguyễn Minh Phan

Crystal caves

By Bao Phi

Crystal Caves in Wisconsin was one of those places, like the Dells or the Shrine Circus or Disneyland, that all the other kids talked about going to with their families during vacations. My parents either didn't have the money or the time or both. My daughter knows this as we drive there together. It's fine, I tell her, even though it was hard when I was a kid, we were fine. I wanted all of these things, sure - but at some point I realized that I would never see this things, only hear about them, to the point where it didn't faze me. It was like another world out there that I could never be a part of, but that was OK. We were OK. Happy sometimes, even. My parents worked so hard.

If there is a gift shop maybe you can pick something out for yourself so you'll always remember you could go today, my daughter says.

I want to tell her that the only reason I don't stop the car and run off into one of these fields alternating between tree and green and wildflower and big blue sky to disappear forever is her.

But I just say, being able to go with you today is enough.

In the cave she holds my hand and says watch your head, don't bang it on headache rock, like the tour guide says. There is a pillar where you walk around it once for good luck, but any more than that brings bad luck.

There is a cave studded with coins - they used to let people stick a coin and make a wish before they were told this was bad for cave ecology. My daughter makes a wish, and tells me she wishes that her daddy would never get angry with her anymore.

Last week I told my therapist I lost my temper and raised my voice with my child and hated myself for it. She told me research shows the human brain doesn't fully develop for 26 years.

We stop in another cave where tiny stalactites thread their way down from the ceiling. The guide says it takes them twenty five years to grow one inch. On the long way home my daughter says she feels like she is lucky and her wish is coming true because I haven't been angry with her all day. I look out to the shallow humpback of a creek, the ribbon of a road past green stalagmites of corn, the blue of the sky that makes me feel so small, like it should.

FORGOTTEN SILENCES AND MILITARIZED MEMORIES

ភាពស្ងប់ស្ងាត់ដែលត្រូវបានគេបំភ្លេចចោល និង អនុស្សាវរីយ៍ក្រោមរបបយោធា

June Kuoch, 21
Los Angeles, CA

Image courtesy of June Kuoch

It was a rainy November day; my mother had taken the twenty-five-minute drive down 35-W from my childhood home to my college apartment. After consuming a larger than holy bowl of Vietnamese Phở in Frogtown, a formerly predominantly black neighborhood that was pushed out by white supremacy which allowed new Southeast Asian refugees to have an ethnic hub. While having small talk about my future life prospects, we took shelter in the car from the rain. Wet we sat on the pleather of our white Toyota Corolla, the atmosphere around us beginning to change. She abruptly went into a quick and precise rant around my father's movie taste.

My parents always had a strenuous relationship. I never really made anything of it while I was a child — I thought my life was normal. Did you know the Khmer Rouge practice forced marriages? They would arrange a marriage to separate families and stop the possibility for political dissent. It's hard to challenge a regime when you and your spouse speak different languages. My parents didn't have that type of marriage, but the diaspora creates a weird recirculation of such occurrences. Some would say my parents had an arranged marriage. They were two Khmer-Chan refugees looking to start a family. Things were amicable, but resentment grows like an invasive species.

That past week in our home, a shelter from the flow of militarized life. My father watched *First, They Killed My Father*. This may seem quite mundane to most, why does it matter he just watched the new hit Netflix movie? For my mother, the war is like a bullet lodged in your spine. It's something you must forever carry, because to take out the cartridge will leave most paralyzed. My disobedience would be a cattle prod to back pains. Story of trauma are thrown knives of subjugation.

Attempting to hide the disdain in her voice, she pushed the air out of her lungs saying,

"I don't understand why he would want to watch that, we should just leave tough things like that in the past… Forgotten. I understand why June would want to watch it. So they can understand what we went through."

Those words really struck me. I was taken aback. My mother has never talked so candidly about her time in childhood, adolescents, or the atrocities in Cambodia. And, I shit you not that is what she said verbatim; I have played back this moment me in my mind like a VHS of *Mulan* in a young Asian American home. My mother's words felt like a fleeting skeleton key to the altar of my ancestors. She refused to let me in, but I still must find my own way into the crypt.

We should leave tough things like that in the past…Forgotten.

I was in my last year of college, a senior, majoring in sociology. We are taught to use and expand our world by using our "sociological imagination", but how can you imagine what is unspoken? Imagine, how do you imagine the reality of your own creation? War and trauma run through me like bacteria in your gut. Our embodied practices, as children of Southeast Asian refugees, is one brought up by the management of a militarized life.

My mother who survived the Khmer Rouge doesn't wish to talk about what occurred, but we as her children must know our history. But, how can we dwell in the archive that is entombed by loss? Yet, my father, her husband, attempts to remember his past through the stories of his fellow survivors brought her so much trauma and sorrow. Thus, we are stuck at a crossroads. We, Southeast Asian Youth, must know the unknowable. We must build bridges of memory without the foundation of history. We must honor our ancestors, yet never know their names. As my mother's child I will not press her on the question of her past. Refugee redress does not just come with resettlement. For me, remembrance can rectify a sense of loss, but for my mother it is the trigger to a bomb of memories she wishes to stay in the crypt. So, I seek alternative sources to understand my familial archive.

PLANTING SEADS   SOUTHEAST ASIAN DIASPORA STORIES

127

ផូន គួច, 21
Los Angeles, CA

នៅថ្ងៃមួយ មានភ្លៀងធ្លាក់ឥតស្រាកស្រាន្ត ក្នុងខែវិច្ឆិកា; ម្ដាយរបស់ខ្ញុំបានបើកឡានចំនួនម្ភៃប្រាំនាទី ចុះទៅផ្លូវ 35-W ចេញពី ផ្ទះនៃកុមារភាពរបស់ខ្ញុំ ទៅផ្ទះល្វែងនៃមហាវិទ្យាល័យ។ បន្ទាប់ពីបរិភោគគុយទាវវៀតណាមមួយចានយ៉ាងធំហួសមាឌ នៅក្នុងក្រុង Frogtown ដែលពីមុនជាភូមិឋាននៃជនជាតិស្បែកខ្មៅរស់នៅច្រើន ដែលត្រូវបានច្រានចេញដោយបរិមានុភាព នៃសាសន៍ស្បែកស ដែលអនុញ្ញាតឲ្យជនភៀសខ្លួនមកពីអាស៊ីអាគ្នេយ៍ ដើម្បីមានមណ្ឌលជាតិពន្ធមួយ។ ក្នុងខណៈមានការនិយាយគ្នាតិចតួចអំពីទស្សនៈ នៃជីវិតរបស់ខ្ញុំនៅអនាគត យើងក៏បានជ្រកនៅក្នុងឡាន កុំឲ្យទទឹកភ្លៀង។ យើងបានអង្គុយនៅលើកៅអីឡានសើមៗ ធ្វើពីក្រណាត់ដូច ស្បែកនៃឡាន Toyota Corolla ពណ៌សរបស់យើង រីឯបរិយាកាសនៅជុំវិញយើងកំពុងផ្លាស់ប្ដូរខ្លាំងណាស់។ ជារំពេចនោះ គាត់បានបែរទៅជានិយាយឡូឡាភ្លាមៗ និងច្បាស់ៗ នៅជុំវិញរសជាតិខ្សែភាពយន្ត នៃឪពុករបស់ខ្ញុំ។

ឪពុកម្ដាយរបស់ខ្ញុំ តែងតែមានទំនាក់ទំនងដ៏ខ្លាំងក្លាជានិច្ច។ ខ្ញុំពិតជាមិនដែលបានធ្វើអ្វី ក្នុងខណៈខ្ញុំនៅក្មេងឡើយ – ខ្ញុំបាន គិតពីជីវិតរបស់ខ្ញុំថាជាធម្មតា។ តើអ្នកបានដឹង ថាខ្មែរក្រហមអនុវត្តការរៀបអាពាហ៍ពិពាហ៍ដោយបង្ខំ ឬទេ? គេនឹងរៀបចំអាពាហ៍ពិពាហ៍ មួយ ដើម្បីបំបែកគ្រួសារ និងបញ្ឈប់លទ្ធភាពសំរាប់ការខ្វែងយោបល់នឹងនយោបាយ។ វាពិបាកដើម្បីប្រឆាំងនឹងរបបមួយ នៅពេលអ្នក និងប្តីប្រពន្ធរបស់អ្នក និយាយភាសាខុសគ្នា។ ឪពុកម្ដាយរបស់ខ្ញុំ ពុំមានអាពាហ៍ពិពាហ៍ប្រភេទនោះឡើយ ប៉ុន្តែការខ្វាត់ព្រាត់ បង្កើតនូវ ការសាយភាយចំឡែកឡើងវិញ នូវការកើតឡើងដូច្នោះ។ អ្នកខ្លះនឹងនិយាយថា ឪពុកម្ដាយរបស់ខ្ញុំ មានអាពាហ៍ពិពាហ៍ដែលបានផ្សំផ្គុំ។ ពួកគាត់គឺជាជនភៀសខ្លួនខ្មែរ-ចាមពីរនាក់ កំពុងតែចាប់ផ្ដើមជាគ្រួសារមួយ។ អ្វីៗមានមេត្រីភាព ប៉ុន្តែការតូចចិត្តលូតលាស់ឡើង ដូចជាជំពូកអ្វីមួយដែលលុកលុយ។

នៅក្នុងផ្ទះរបស់យើងនៅអាទិត្យកន្លងមកនោះ ជម្រកមួយចេញពីការហូរនៃជីវិតយោធា។ ឪពុករបស់ខ្ញុំបានមើលភាពយន្តមួយរឿង ជាដំបូង គេបានសំឡាប់ឪពុករបស់ខ្ញុំ។ ការនេះហាក់ដូចជាសាមញ្ញណាស់ សំរាប់មនុស្សភាគច្រើន ថាតើហេតុអ្វីជារឿងសំខាន់ ដែលគាត់គ្រាន់តែបានមើលភាពយន្តថ្មីរបស់ Netflix? សំរាប់ម្ដាយរបស់ខ្ញុំវិញ សង្គ្រាមគឺបីដូចគ្រាប់កំភ្លើងបានជាប់នៅក្នុងឆ្អឹងខ្នង របស់ខ្ញុំ។ វាគឺជាអ្វីៗដែលអ្នកត្រូវតែស្ពាយជាប់ជាដរាប ពីព្រោះដើម្បីយកចេញពីឡូតគ្រាប់កំភ្លើង នឹងទុកឲ្យមនុស្សភាគច្រើនពិការ។ ការមិនស្ដាប់បង្គាប់របស់ខ្ញុំ នឹងបីដូចជាយកជន្លួញមកចាក់គោឲ្យឈឺខ្នង។ រឿងនៃសេចក្ដីស្លុតរន្ធត់ ហាក់បីដូចជាគេបានចោលកាំបិតមកលើព្រោះនៅក្រោមអំណាចគេ។

ការប៉ុនប៉ងដើម្បីលាក់បាំងការមាក់ងាយ នៅក្នុងសំឡេងរបស់គាត់ នោះគាត់បានបញ្ចេញខ្យល់ចេញពីសួតរបស់គាត់ ដោយនិយាយថា

"ខ្ញុំមិនយល់ពីហេតុអ្វីដែលគាត់ចង់មើលភាពយន្តនោះយើងគួរតែចាកចេញពីអ្វីៗដែលពិបាកៗយ៉ាងដូចនោះ ក្នុងអតីតកាល ...បំភ្លេចចោលទៅ។ ខ្ញុំយល់ពីមូលហេតុដែលផូន ចង់មើលវា។ ដូច្នេះ គេអាចយល់ពីអ្វីៗដែលយើងបានឆ្លងកាត់"។

ពាក្យទាំងនោះពិតជាពាធាខ្ញុំ។ ខ្ញុំត្រូវបានស្រឡាំងកាំង។ ម្ដាយរបស់ខ្ញុំ មិនដែលបាននិយាយដោយឥតលាក់លៀមម្ដេ៉ះ អំពីពេលរបស់គាត់ក្នុងវ័យកុមារ តរុណវ័យ ឬអំពើឃោឃៅ នៅកម្ពុជាឡើយ។ ហើយខ្ញុំមិនប៉ងបោកអ្នកទេ ថាអ្វីៗដែលគាត់បាននិយាយជាពាក្យពិត; ខ្ញុំបានលេងឈុតនេះម្ដងទៀត

នៅក្នុងចិត្តរបស់ខ្ញុំ ដូចជា VHS នៃ *Mulan* នៅក្នុងផ្ទះពូកក្មេងៗនៃអាស៊ី-អាមេរិកាំង។ ពាក្យរបស់ម្តាយខ្ញុំ បានមានអារម្មណ៍ហាក់ដូចជាតន្លើនំរោងឆ្លើងដែលឈឺឈឹឈប់ៗ ចំពោះអាស្មា នៃបុព្វជនរបស់ខ្ញុំ។ គាត់បានបជិសេធឲ្យខ្ញុំចូល ប៉ុន្តែខ្ញុំនៅតែត្រូវតែរកមធ្យោបាយដោយខ្លួនឯង ចូលទៅក្នុងបន្ទប់អាថ៌កំបាំង។

យើងគួរតែទុកចោលនូវអ្វីដែលពិបាកយ៉ាងដូចនោះ ក្នុងអតីតកាល...បំភ្លេចចោលទៅ។

ជាឆ្នាំចុងក្រោយរបស់ខ្ញុំនៅមហាវិទ្យាល័យ ជានិស្សិតជើងចាស់ វិស័យសំខាន់ខាងសង្គមវិទ្យា។ យើងត្រូវបានបង្រៀន ម្យ្រាប្រើ និងពន្លឹកពិភពលោករបស់យើង ដោយប្រើ "ការស្រមៃខាងសង្គមវិទ្យា" ប៉ុន្តែឥឡូវនេះ តើអ្នកអាចស្រមៃពីអ្វីដែលមិនបាននិយាយឬទេ? ស្រមៃទៅមើល តើអ្នកស្រមៃភាពពិត នៃការបង្កើតដោយខ្លួនឯង ដោយដូចម្តេច? សង្គ្រាម និងសេចក្តីស្ងូតរន្ធត់ ឆ្លងកាត់តាមខ្ញុំដូចជាមេរោគ បាក់តេរី នៅក្នុងពោះវៀនរបស់អ្នក។ ការអនុវត្តន៍ក្នុងរូបកាយរបស់យើង ហាន៖ជាក្មេងៗនៃជនភៀសខ្លួនមក ពីអាស៊ីអាគ្នេយ៍ គឺជាអ្នកដែល បានបីបាច់តាមការចាត់ចែងនៃជីវិតយោបា។

ម្តាយរបស់ខ្ញុំបាននៅរស់ ពីសម័យខ្មែរក្រហម មិនប្រាថ្នានិយាយអំពីអ្វីដែលបានកើតឡើងទេ ប៉ុន្តែយើងជាកូនៗរបស់គាត់ ត្រូវរើ ដឹងប្រវត្តិសាស្រ្តរបស់យើង។ ប៉ុន្តែ តើយើងអាចរស់នៅក្នុង ឯកសារសំខាន់ ដែលបានរក់ដោយការបាត់បង់ ដោយដូចម្តេច? មិនតែប៉ុណ្ណោះ ឱពុករបស់ខ្ញុំ ជាស្វាមីរបស់ម្តាយខ្ញុំ ប៉ុនប៉ងលើកឡើករឿងពីអតីតកាល តាមរយៈរឿងនិទាន ពីគ្រួសារបស់គាត់ដែលនៅរស់ ដែលបាននាំគាត់ឲ្យ មានសេចក្តីស្ងូតព្រួយ ជាអនេក។ ដូច្នេះហើយ យើងបានជាប់នៅឆ្លងផ្លូវប្រសព្វឆ្លយ។ យើងជាកូនៗវ័យវ័យអាស៊ីអាគ្នេយ៍ ត្រូវតែ ស្ពាល់អ្វីដែលមិនអាចស្ពាល់បាន។ យើងត្រូវតែកសាងស្ថានៃអនុស្សាវរីយ៍ ដោយគ្មានគ្រឹះនៃ ប្រវត្តិសាស្រ្ត។ យើងត្រូវតែគោរពបូជន របស់យើង តែមិនដែលស្ពាល់ឈ្មោះរបស់គេឡើយ។ ហាន៖ជាកូននៃម្តាយរបស់ខ្ញុំ ខ្ញុំនឹងមិនឈ្លៀចស្ងួសសំណួរគាត់ អំពីអតីតកាលរបស់ គាត់ទេ។ ដំណើរវិវេកជនភៀសខ្លួន មិនមែនត្រាន់តែមកជាមួយនឹងកំរាល់នៅឡើងវិញឡើងឡើយ។ សំរាប់ខ្ញុំវិញ ការនឹកចាំអាចកើតម្រង់និច្ច័យនៃការបាត់បង់ ប៉ុន្តែសំរាប់ម្តាយរបស់ខ្ញុំវិញ គឺជាកែធ្វើឲ្យផ្ទះគ្រាប់បែកនៃអនុ ស្សាវរីយ៍ ដែលគាត់ប្រាថ្នាឲ្យនៅក្នុងបន្ទប់អាថ៌កំបាំង។ ដូច្នេះខ្ញុំស្ងេងរកប្រភពជនទៅៗត ដើម្បីឲ្យយល់ដឹង កសារសំខាន់នៃគ្រួសាររបស់ខ្ញុំ។

Illustration by Christina Sayaovong Vang

NO TEARS COULD COME OUT

Quaj Tsis Los Kua Muag

*Pa Lee, 99
Saint Paul

I was born June 1919 in a village outside of Xieng Khouang, Laos during French colonization in Southeast Asia. During the time of French occupation in Laos, we saw many people in our village selling their children to foreigners. Many of the villagers were too poor to support all their children, and saw that as the only option. We regularly witnessed the persecution of locals who spoke out against the foreigners. It was a sad and fearful time to be living in Laos. Our family fled to the northern region of Vietnam for safety. I gave birth to my first child in Vietnam. When the French finally left, we heard from others that Vang Pao was protecting Hmong villages and decided it would be safe to bring our family back to Laos.

Those who came to America when they were young or were born here only hear stories. They didn't have to live through what we experienced. When the war broke out, I remembered what it was like to see the bombs dropped from the planes. We were out gardening when they fell. They landed on the ground with a loud "BOOM" and clouds of red dust and dirt emerged everywhere. We ran and looked back to see what was happening. We couldn't look away at the bombardment. The sky had suddenly turned bright red. Bombshells and casings were everywhere on the ground. They scraped our feet as we ran away to try to escape the explosions. Many homes in our village were completely blown up with people still inside them. Everywhere we looked we saw parts of the village torn up into shreds. We were terrified and in complete shock. The bombs were so close to killing us. Even if we wanted to cry, no tears could come out.

We knew we couldn't stay in the village for much longer, so we ran into the jungle. We carried the children on our backs and swam across the Mekong. Our older uncle was our guide. I tied myself with some rope and threw a hemp basket behind me for my husband to hang onto. The Mekong river was wide with fast rapids. Our whole family had to tie ourselves to each other to swim across the river. If we hadn't tied ourselves like that, we would have drowned. We were refugees and moved to Phanat Nikhom in February 1981 where we stayed for one month. Shortly after arriving there, we were sponsored by a Lutheran church. By March, we landed in Michigan.

I've witnessed a lot in my 99 years. It's often hard to reflect back on those times because they are so heartbreaking. It was scary and unfortunate what we went through. I'm very grateful to be in America, and really fortunate for the government's support over the years. I think if we had stayed back in Laos, things would have turned out very differently. For instance, I don't think I'd still be alive. I appreciate the times when we can all come together to share our stories. Even though there are many different ethnic groups present in America from Southeast Asia, we had similar experiences during that tragic era.

It fills my heart with joy that we're alive today and planting seeds for the future.

———

*Paj Lis, 99
Saint Paul

Kuv yug rau xyoo 1919, rau ib lub zos tawm ntawm xeev Xieng Khouang, Nplog teb. Thaum no yog thaum uas Fabkis tuaj kav teb kav chaw nyob rau sab Southeast Asia. Lub sij hawm thaum cov Fabkis tau tuaj kav teb chaws Nplog, muaj neeg ntau heev uas nyob rau hauv peb lub zos tau muab lawv cov menyuam muag rau cov neeg ua tuaj sab nraum Nplog tuaj. Feem coob ntawm peb lub zej zog cov tib neeg ces txom nyem heev, thiab tsis muaj peev xwm yuav los tu tau tag nrho lawv cov me nyuam. Muab lawv cov menyuam muag ces tsuas yog tib txoj kev lawm pom lawm xwb. Peb yeej pom tas li qhov uas lawv ntes cov pej xeem uas tau tawm suab txog cov uas tuaj sab nraum Nplog tuaj. Nws yog ib lub sij hawm uas tu siab thiab txaus ntshai heev nyob rau hauv Nplog teb. Kuv tsev neeg peb thiaj tau khiav mus nyob rau qaum teb Nyab Laj, kom dim kev phom sij. Kuv yug kuv thawj tug me nyuam nyob rau Nyab Laj teb. Thaum peb hnov tias cov Fabkis taum tawm lawm, peb kuj tau hnov tias Nai Phoo Vaj Pov nws los tiv thaiv peb cov zos Hmoob. Peb thiaj li xav tias tej zaum yuav nyab xeeb lawm yog peb rov qab mus nyob rau Nplog teb.

Cov ua tuaj rau lub teb chaws Meskas teb thaum lawv tseem yau losis tuaj yug tim Meskas, lawv tsuas hnov neej neeg xwb. Lawv tsis tau pom thiab ntsib cov peb tau dhau los. Thaum tsov rog tawg, kuv nco tau tias cov foob pob uas dav hlau tau tso los zoo li cas. Peb tseem tab tom ua teb thaum foob pob poob los rau hauv av. Ces cov foob pob tau tawg nrov "BOOM". Huab liab nrog rau av tawm pes zaws los. Peb tau khiav thiab saib qab seb yog dab tsi tshwm sim. Peb ces cia li saib ntsoov cov foob pob uas poob los. Lub ntuj cia li hloov mus ua xim liab ploog. Tej me plhaub foob pob ces poob pawg lug nyob rau hauv av. Cov plhaub foob pob ces kuam thiab hlais peb tej taw thaum peb khiav. Muaj ntau lub tsev uas nyob rau peb lub zos, txawm hais tias tseem muaj neeg nyob hauv los, ces cia li tawg tag. Ntsia qhov twg los peb lub zos ces ntuag thiab tawg tag li lawm. Peb tau ntshai thiab ceeb loj heev. Tshuav me me xwb ces cov foob poob twb tawg raug peb lawm thiab. Lub sij hawm no, txawm hais tias peb xav quaj los yeej tsis los kua muag li lawm.

Peb yeej paub lawm hais tias peb yuav nyob tsis tau rau hauv peb lub zos ntev lawm, peb thiaj li tau khiav mus nkaum rau hav zoov hav tsuag. Peb ev peb cov menyuam rau saum nruab qaum thiab ua luam dej hla tus dej Nab Khoom. Peb tus txiv ntxawm yog tus coj peb kev. Kuv tau muab kuv tus kheej khi nrog ib co hlua thiab ev ib lub pob tawb kom kuv tus txiv tuav tau. Tus dej nab khoom dav thiab muaj ceem heev li. Peb tau muab hlua khi tag nrho peb tsev neeg mas peb thiaj li hla dhau. Yog hais tias peb tsis khi ces ntshe peb twb poob dej tuag tag lawm. Peb tau los yog neeg poob teb chaws thiab tau los nyob Phanat Nikhom rau thaum pib xyoo 1981. Peb nyob ntawv tau ib hlis nkaus. Thaum peb nyuam qhuav los txog Phanat Nikhom tsis ntev xwb, peb twb raug xaiv los ntawm ib lub Lutheran Church. Nyob rau thaum lub caij Ntuj

Tshiab, xyoo 1981 ces peb tuaj txog teb chaws Meskas.

Kuv nyob los tau 99 xyoos no, kuv tau pom ntau tsav ntau yam. Tej thaum yog kuv rov qab xav mus txog tej sib hawm ntawv mas, nws nyuab heev li, vim nws muaj kev tu siab ntau heev li. Cov uas peb tau dhau los mas txaus ntshai thiab tsis muaj hmoo kiag li. Tab sis, kuv zoo siab uas kuv tau tuaj nyob rau teb chaws Meskas no, thiab kuv muaj hmoo heev uas cov nov tswv Meskas tau pab kuv los tau ntau lub xyoo no. Kuv xav hais tias ntshe yog kuv tseem nyob tim Nplog teb, txhua yam txhua tsav yuav txawv deb heev li. Ntshe kuv twb tsis muaj sia nyob lawm los kuj muaj. Kuv xav ua tsaug rau lub sij hawm uas peb tau muaj rau peb sawv daws los piav peb zaj neej neeg.Txawm hais tias yuav muaj ntau haiv neeg nyob rau Meskas teb uas tuaj tim Southeast Asia tuaj, los peb sawv daws yeej ntsib thiab pom ntau yam uas zoo ib yam rau lub caij nyoog tu siab ntawv.

Kuv zoo siab heev hais tias hnub no peb sawv daws tseem muaj txoj sia nyob, thiab peb tau los cog peb cov noob rau yav pem suab.

*Name and identifiers have been changed under storyteller's request.

WHAT'S THE GIFT YOU WANT TO PASS ON TO THE NEXT GENERATION?

Curiosity and eagerness to learn and embrace our cultures — food, language, and (shared) histories.

ABOUT THE AUTHORS

Chanida Phaengdara Potter

Chanida Phaengdara Potter is a 1.5 Lao American refugee, mother, amplifier and narrative storyteller. She's the founding editor of Little Laos on the Prairie and executive director of The SEAD Project. She has a BA in Global Studies and Media Studies from the University of Minnesota and an MPA from Hamline University. Chanida lives in Minneapolis, Minnesota with her husband, two children and snowbirding parents.

mk nguyễn

mk is a second generation Viet mother in Mni Sota based in the Frogtown neighborhood of Saint Paul, Minnesota. She loves talking to people about regeneration of peoplehood and planet. She draws strength from the bumblebee. She learns about her world through cross pollination. She takes sweet nectar from every flower she comes to know and shares nectar across her network to help each flower grow.

Narate Keys

Narate Keys is a mother, Cambodian poet and spoken word artist based in Saint Paul, Minnesota. She is the self-published author of *The Good Life*. Her family lived through the Khmer Rouge genocide in Cambodia and she was born in a Thai refugee camp. Keys writes to express the true meaning of her voice. It is through poetry that Keys has found love, appreciation, and encouragement.

Pheng Thao

Pheng Thao is part of the 1.5 generation from Laos and is a mental health practitioner who is the founding director of ManForward and a Hmong men's program called Txivneej Yawg. He facilitates trainings to several local, national, and international organizations on gender based violence including domestic violence, sex trafficking, and sexual violence. Pheng also coordinates Men and Masculine Folks Network, a collaborative network of community organizations and individuals. Pheng serves as a trustee on the Minnesota Women's Foundation and is a 2018 Bush Fellow. Pheng lives in Saint Paul, Minnesota with his partner and son.

GLOSSARY OF TERMS

Words, concepts, names and locations that have appeared in our stories and conversations.

Ban Vinai Refugee Camp

A refugee camp site that was opened from 1975 until 1992 in the Pak Chom District of Loei province in Thailand. At its peak there were 45,000 Hmong and other highland people who fled from Laos living in Ban Vinai. Other major refugee camps in Thailand included Chiangkham, Na Pho, Nam Yao, Nong Khai, Sikhiu, Songkhla and Ubon.

Chao Fa

Hmong resistance faction formed after Pathet Lao and communist soldiers clashed with Hmong villages. Many Chao Fa fled their homes and hid in the jungles of Laos to avoid persecution from Pathet Lao. Although most Chao Fa have resettled, it is estimated there are still up to 3,000 Chao Fa families still hiding and fighting in the jungles of Laos (UNPO).

Diaspora

1. Collective experience of people who were displaced due to political, economic, social systems, with affiliation and connections in both country of residence and country of origin (Parrenas & Siu) 2. Populations, such as members of an ethnic or religious group that originated in the same place but dispersed to different locations (Britannica). 3. A sense of belonging to more than one history, to more than one time and place, to more than one past and future (Docker).

Fawn/Fon

A traditional Lao way of dancing using the bending of hands while in movement.

Ho Chi Minh Trail

During the Vietnam War, a trail leading through North Vietnam, Laos and Cambodia into South Vietnam to provide troops, supplies, weapons and ammunition to forces fighting the South Vietnamese and their allies.

Kampuchea (Cambodia)

A Southeast Asian country with more than 16 million people. The Khmer are indigenous people of Cambodia and is home to numerous ethnic groups including Việt, Chinese, Khmer Loeu, and Cham. It was once the Kingdom of Angkor. In the 12th century, the Khmer Empire was the largest empire of Southeast Asia.

Khmer Rouge

A communist guerrilla organization that began in the 1960s under the leadership of Pol Pot that engaged in civil war with the Cambodian government in 1970, seizing power in 1975, instituting Year Zero, a program to restore Cambodia to the glory of the Angkor era, resulting in the massacre of millions of Cambodians before the Khmer Rouge were driven out of power.

Laos

A Southeast Asian country with more than 6 million people. It borders all of the Mekong River in Southeast Asia and is the only country accessible to Thailand, Cambodia and Việtnam. It is rich in mountains, forests and natural resources. The Khmu are indigenous people of Laos and is home to over 50 ethnic groups including Lao, Hmong, Tai Dam, Phutai and Iu Mien. It was once the Kingdom of Lan Xang (Land of a Million Elephants) and the folktale of Prince Sinxay and Nak (Dragon Snake) protected its land from outside invasion.

Laotian

Frequently used as an inclusive term for people with roots in Laos, including ethnic Lao, Khmu, Tai Dam, Iu Mien, Hmong, and others.

Mni Sota

Indigenous term for the region presently known as the state of Minnesota.

Nyob Zoo
Greeting in Hmong language. Transliteration is: Hello, be well.

Paj Ntaub
Hmong embroidery with designs that are inspired by nature such as mountains, birds, trees, butterflies, flowers, and the sun. Paj Ntaub appears most commonly on traditional Hmong clothing, baby carriers, hats, and story cloths.

Pathet Lao (Ai Nong)
Formed in 1950, the Pathet Lao movement aligned itself with the Viet Minh against French rule in Indochina, and took control of Laos in 1975.

Phanat Nikhom Transition Refugee Camp
A transition refugee camp site opened from 1980 until mid-1990s in the Phanat Nikhom district of Chonburi province in Thailand. Many Việt, Hmong, Lao, and Khmer were temporarily held at Phanat while waiting for their sponsorship papers to be approved to resettle in a third country.

Phnom Penh
The current capital of Cambodia.

Refugee
A resilient and strong group of people, forced from their homelands because they are unable or unwilling to return to their country of origin due to a founded fear of persecution. Typically due to race, religion, nationality, membership of a particular social group or political opinion.

Royal Lao Army
The land branch of the Lao armed forces under the Lao monarchy during the mid-20th century. There was also a Royal Lao Air Force and a Royal Lao Navy.

Sabaidee (ສະບາຍດີ)
Greeting in Lao language. A typical transliteration is: Hello, good health to you.

Saigon
Capital of South Việt Nam, from 1954 to 1976. It was considered the "Pearl of the Orient" by French colonial standards.

Samana (Labor Camp)
Labor camp/re-education camps where the people of Laos who were part of the former Royal government were subjected into intensive hard labor and political indoctrination after the Fall of Vientiane.

Secret War
A proxy war fought in the mid-20th century between Cold War-era superpowers. The US Central Intelligence Agency with the assistance of the US State Department organized a secret army in Laos composed of highland cultures to agitate North Việt and Pathet Lao forces using the Ho Chi Minh Trail. The Secret War is largely considered to have ended between 1973-1975 with the withdrawal of US paramilitary advisors and the end of the secret bombing campaign in Laos called Operation Barrel Roll (1964-1973) designed to disrupt activity along the Ho Chi Minh Trail.

Southeast Asia (Indochina)
The specific mainland Southeast Asian countries of Cambodia, Laos and Việtnam that share the Mekong River and geopolitical region of Asia identified by shared history of French colonization and US military intervention.

Suostei (សួស្ដី)
Greeting in Khmer language.

Vang Pao (Variation General Vang Pao, GVP)
Vang Pao was a major general in the Royal Lao Army and is commonly referred to as "Tsiv" or 'the father of modern Hmong politics and leadership'. He was the general of the CIA Hmong Guerilla forces in Laos, and a critical public figure that influenced the repatriation of thousands of Hmong to the United States from 1975 through the 2000s.

Vientiane
The current capital of Laos (Lao PDR), and capital of the former Kingdom of Laos since 1563.

Việt Kiều
A term used to describe people of the Việt diaspora who live outside of Việt Nam.

Việt Minh
A national independence coalition formed by Hồ Chí Minh on his birthday, May 19, in 1941.

Việt Nam (Vietnam)
An "S" shaped peninsula, cradled by the South China Sea. This land been called many names. It was commonly known as Annam until 1945, when both the imperial government in Huế and Việt Minh government in Hanoi both recognized it as Việt Nam. It holds 54 ethnic groups, with the Kinh people occupying 86 % of the population. According to Kinh folklore, the people on this land originated from fairies and dragons.

Việt Nam War
A historical period taught in United States schools and media to describe the violent conflict that erupted in Việt Nam,Laos, and Cambodia from 1 November 1st, 1955 to 30 April 30th, 1975.

Wat
Theravada Buddhist temple, used in Khmer, Lao and Thai languages.

Xin Chào
A humble greeting in Việt language.

ACKNOWLEDGEMENTS

The journey to produce this historic book has been beautifully engaging, healing, humbling and challenging at the same time. It's not without our village of supporters that this journey to get where we are has been possible. We are grateful to our interpreters, translators, volunteers, artists and community members who came to our community conversations to share space and their vulnerabilities with us. Thank you for being part of the necessary, courageous and intentional work to carve out new possibilities and make our Southeast Asian Minnesotan narratives more visible.

We are immensely grateful to the young people of The SEAD Project. First, Ze Thao, who has been a coordinating force as well as a wonderful writer. Bryan Thao Worra for being our on-call legendary writer and all things historic. Amanda Nguyễn, Maikha Khang, Lê Văn Tigana, Tiffany Nguyễn; who are raising us as much as we're raising them. They worked tirelessly to gather interviews, hold conversations with elders and craft stories.

We have deep appreciation for Dara Beevas and the Wise Ink team's expertise, care and professionalism in helping us navigate the publishing world.

To everyone who has been part of everything from the beginning, including creating art, capturing film, transcribing voice recordings, translating stories, interpreting, planning, facilitating, healing and being together as community; we are indebted to your contributions and commitment to the memories we shared. This includes Aloun Phoulavan, Angelina Trâm Nguyễn, Ayo Clemons and the People's Movement Center, Banlang Phoummasouvanh, Bao Phi, Bee Vang-Moua, Bounlieng Daoheuang, Center for Social Healing, Ched Nin, Christina Vang, Christopher Khounbanam, Dean Tan, Duong Nhu Ha, Eastside Freedom Library, Ha Vo, Hun H. and You H., Huynh Thi Lanh, Jason Rolan, Jay Rattanavong, Jessica Pham, Joshua Dyrud, June Kuoch, Kat Eng, Kaysone Syonesa, Kevin Yang, Khou Vue, Kirk MacKinnon Morrow and the Minnesota Humanities Center, Kith Khounbanam, Lar Munstrock, Leyan Trang, ManForward, Manola Suvannarad, Michael Sasorith, Neng Shao Yang, Nguyen Minh Phan, Nguyen Tran, Nouth Phaengdara, Oanh Vu, Pa Houa Chang, Pa Lee*, Pele Le, Phillipe Thao, Risa Ya, Sam S.*, Sandy Ci Moua, Sang Truong, Sethey Ben, Sia Thao, Sky Bui*, Somongkol Teng, Thaiphy Phan-Quang, Tong Kou Thao, Tzianeng Vang, Virak Soth and the many more supporters and friends who carried us to this milestone.

ຂອບໃຈ. cảm ơn. ua tsaug. អរគុណ. Thank you.

Chanida Phaengdara Potter, mk nguyen, Pheng Thao and Narate Keys